Photo credits:
Front cover: Black Star: Gene Daniels; **Back cover: AP/Wide World Photos, Inc.** (top right, center right, center left); **Sygma** (top left), Gene Spatz (bottom right), Randy Taylor (bottom left).

Pictured on back cover: Charles Manson (top left), Theodore "Ted" Bundy (top right), Ed Gein (center left), Jeffrey Dahmer (center right), Wayne Williams (bottom left), weapons owned by David Berkowitz (bottom right).

Contributing writers: Briggs Adams, Bill G. Cox, Jacob Drake, Bill Francis, William J. Helmer, Gary C. King, Julie Malear, David Nemec, Charles Pelkie, Samuel Roen, Billie Francis Taylor, Joyce Werges.

CONTENTS

CONTENTS

FOREWORD

Murder. Has it become acceptable or is it an aberration? It is commonplace in our cities. It happens in war. We execute known killers. Irrational dictators are silenced. We are accustomed to killing.

But there are times when the most hardened heart reacts to the sickening twistedness of the abject criminal mind. It is one thing, we think, to kill, but another to murder a man and then serve him up for dinner with carrots and onions. When the criminal mind goes beyond the pale to butchering, cannibalizing, and terrorizing, a line is crossed. The sheer number of victims can make us sit up and take notice. Let it be murder *and* sexual perversion and the headlines will scream at you in outrage. Add dismemberment, we are repulsed. The victim is a child, we weep in disbelief. Our proclivity toward numbness dissipates in the wake of shocking reality.

For most people, emotions are kept in check. They will take that deep breath. Count to ten. Walk away. But what about the mind that can't learn the sequence. Emotion and intelligence gone awry. It is no longer murder, it is murder with a sadistic twist. Creativity put into bizarre forms of inhumanity.

The case histories in this volume are about the murderers who went one irrevocable step beyond, into the taboo realms of the human psyche.

MURDER
AND
MAYHEM

MORE THAN 75 CASE HISTORIES OF HEINOUS CRIMES

INTRODUCTION BY
JAMES ELLROY,
AUTHOR OF
THE BLACK DAHLIA

CONTENTS

James Ellroy is one of America's leading young mystery writers. He wrote *The Black Dahlia*, the best-selling novel based on the sensational 1947 murder of Elizabeth Short in Los Angeles. Mr. Ellroy's knowledge of serial killers and murderers is held in high regard.

Special thanks to Rose Mandelsberg of *True Detective* magazine.

INTRODUCTION

David "Son of Sam" Berkowitz said his neighbor's dog ordered him to kill. Racist Milwaukee homophobe, Jeffrey Dahmer, started his twisted career in high school and soon graduated to a bloodbath/feast of stewed hearts, boiled hands, and chilled heads. They're young; they're bold; to an America egregiously entrenched in the mythology of good versus evil and inundated by slaughter flicks, hideous rock 'n' roll videos, and catastrophic bad news they're strangely groovy.

They're serial killers. They're mass murderers. They're butchers.

The media would have us believe that they lurk on every street corner. In reality, the FBI estimates that perhaps only fifty serial killers exist currently in America. They, along with other murderous misfits, horrify; they inspire dark curiosity; oddly, they seduce. They represent a minuscule percentage of this country's overall homicide rate and capture a maximum amount of national attention. You're much more likely to run into a crazed crack addict devoid of interesting psychology who'll off you for dope cash, but serial killers terrify, tantalize, and titillate—they boogaloo to nightmare Nachtmusick far outside conventional thought—and it is the details of their hellish symbolism that hold us in thrall.

Dig:
Ed Gein, psycho momma's boy, wanted to be a woman. He burgled graves, studied anatomy texts, snuffed a couple of local yokels, and fashioned a woman's dry-cured skin into a vest.

Gary Heidnik, rampant rape-o murderer and electrifying macabre "minister," kept a harem of hapless, helpless women in his basement, chained to his plumbing.

The never captured "Zodiac" killer offered this motive for his slayings, "I'm collecting slaves for my afterlife."

John Wayne Gacy tortured male prostitutes and assorted homosexuals, dressed up as a clown to entertain crippled kids, and served as a minor big cheese in the local Democratic party machine.

Dig the connecting threads—sex and rage—and dig the basis of squarejohn society's fascination with serial killers: they can possess anybody they want, their sexual power is absolute, conscience-less, devoid of ramifications like vulnerability, love, and waiting for the third or fourth date to go to bed.

The genealogy of their madness, exposed in carefully detailed case histories, backlights their epic trauma to such an extent that we are made to feel secure in our more prosaic dysfunction.

Thus we, the "sane" reading/viewing public, seek to stick our hand into the fire, feel the flame, then return to safety. Serial killers have captured our consciousness of late—call them the shock troops of the murderous American 20th century. Call their outré symbolism the hieroglyphics of hell and place them in the front row center context of the book you are about to read—your hand scorched via MURDER.

Dig the cast you are about to meet in a multitude of cameos: Leopold and Loeb, Gary Gilmore, Richard Speck, Charles Whitman, Charlie Manson, Richard "Night Stalker" Ramirez, Martha Beck and Raymond Fernandez, the Hillside Stranglers— murderers most foul, most deranged, most vicious, most pathetic, most significant of the society that has spawned them. Killers most sex-crazed, greedy, impetuous, and inspired by bizarre stimuli. Killers who for one or many brief horrifying moments stood outside all moral strictures imposed by God/Goddess/Human law and stole the lives of those they loved/hated/lusted for/coveted/envied/raged at or just plain grooved on. Killers/murderers/slashers/bludgeoners/ poisoners/shooters/mutilators—pathologically derived detritus that cuts across all gender/ racial/socioeconomic barriers to fascinate us/scare us/make us turn off our reading lights with quaking hands.

Woooooo, daddy-o! Feel the thrust of your curiosity edging you forward, wishing this introduction concluded so that you can get to the stories inside? Do you know what it is that you ultimately wish to know? Do you feel some queasy undertow reaching for you—slithering around your soul, making your blood pump spasmodically and send tingles out your extremities? Are you experiencing a certain ambivalence: The desire to snout in the gutter of twisted psychopathology while remaining morally superior to the fiends you are about to meet on paper?

You are experiencing these things? Good. This means you have a salutary basic curiosity: You want to know why. Frankly, the genealogy of murder is incomprehensible—a patchwork of unfathomable psychology juxtaposed against societal forces grinding away. What a good writer can illuminate are key incidental details to spark his readers' consciousness and thus spawn some inchoate realization of motive/cause and effect.

Digsville, murder mavens/death devotees:

Nathan Leopold and Richard Loeb, 1924 intellectual "thrill killers," possessed 350 I.Q. points between them. Their preferred reading material: horror comic books and rationalist philosophy—Nietzschean ramblings/patriarchal thought—they believed themselves to be super males—rather than the callow buffoons they were.

Mass murderer Richard Speck pulled the plug on eight Chicago nurses while flying high on

Nembutal and Thunderbird wine—a heady brew that may have unlocked lethal instincts that might have remained forever dormant.

Kenneth Bianchi and Angelo Buono, the Hillside Stranglers, were cousins: Bianchi was a quack "psychologist" armed with bogus mail-order diplomas; Buono owned a car reupholstery shop. Antithetical individual personalities, one collective persona: KILLER.

Gary Gilmore, the 1977 "I want to die" killer, sustained possible brain damage from frequent bops on the head. Did physiological dysfunction contribute to his kill spree?

Did Patrick Kearney, a bizarre homosexually oriented serial killer who lurked on Southern California roadways in the early '80s, have some perversely spiritual influence on other psycho roadside killers?

Details.

Ruminations on motive.

A brief treatise on how and why we want to know.

In conclusion: Read the stories inside. Fear the killers; pray for their victims; extend sympathy toward murderers' childhoods. Think of the line between us and them as fragile and in need of jealous guarding.

— *James Ellroy*

MARY FLORA BELL

TEN-YEAR-OLD BELL SMILED AS SHE ASKED TO SEE HER VICTIM IN HIS CASKET.

On May 25, 1968, in Newcastle, England, a four-year-old boy named Martin George Brown was found strangled. The next day, police found a crudely written note in a vandalized nursery school. The note included obscenities and said in part, "We murder, watch out. . . ." Another note discovered by the police included a disturbing statement that "we did murder Martin Brown." On May 30, pretty, dark-haired Mary Flora Bell, then only ten years old, went to the home of Brown's parents and asked with a smile to see him in his casket. On July 31, three-year-old Brian Howe was strangled to death.

The slayings came amid a series of strange happenings. There were reports that Mary Flora Bell had tried to choke two young playmates. When questions began to arise concerning the death of Brian Howe, Mary Bell and her friend Norma Bell (no relation) accused each other of the murders.

The trial of the two girls began December 5,

1968, in Newcastle, England. The Crown claimed that the defendants had killed Brown and Howe. Norma Bell, who was thirteen at the time of the trial, was acquitted in both cases. Mary Bell was convicted not only of choking both boys to death but also of inflicting minor wounds on Howe's stomach and genital area with a scissors and razor blade. The final verdict was manslaughter rather than murder. The jury ruled that Mary had "diminished responsibility" at the time of the attacks on the boys.

Since there was no hospital available at the time that met the requirements of England's Mental Health Act, the judge sentenced Mary to detention for life. She was confined in a correctional institution for boys. Although she was carefully segregated from the boys, many problems arose from this arrangement. The lack of social services or mental institutions to accommodate the child shocked the world and brought a call for reform.

BILLIONAIRE BOYS CLUB
JOE HUNT

COMMITTING TWO COLD-BLOODED MURDERS SMASHED THEIR DREAMS OF UNLIMITED SUCCESS.

Joe Hunt was the handsome, charismatic leader of the Billionaire Boys Club (BBC). The investment confederation of around 30 young men, all from wealthy families, was formed in Los Angeles in 1983. The intention of these men, all in their twenties, was success—making a great deal of money in as little time as possible.

A manifesto Joe Hunt presented at the organizational meeting in March 1983 delineated the Billionaire Boys Club idea. A network of individuals was to be bound together by what he called "Paradox Philosophy." Essentially, this meant taking whatever means was necessary to get what you want. The basic unit of the organization was a "cell" of five members. A BBC business enterprise was called a "shape." A shape's purpose was to wind up with more money than was originally put into it. The leaders of the BBC were called "shadings," who were "the embodiment of Paradox Philosophy." These teachings formed the justification for ruthless, cold-blooded murder.

Hunt first brought murder into the plan when he found out that a Los Angeles con man named Ron Levin—for whom Hunt had invested money in commodities that earned $13 million—had bilked him of his promised half of that windfall. Levin stalled, promising eventual payment. On the evening of June 6, 1984, Joe Hunt and another BBC member, Jim Pittman, supposedly went to Levin's apartment and forced the 42-year-old con man to sign a $1.5-million check drawn on a Swiss bank account. Then they took him into a bedroom, where they executed him with a silenced .25-caliber pistol as he lay facedown on the bed. The two BBC members hauled the body to a previously dug pit in an isolated canyon. Before burying it, they riddled the corpse with shotgun fire to prevent identification.

In the middle of June, a 23-year-old Iranian man, Reza Eslaminia, was introduced into the BBC. He soon proposed a plan to force his father, Hedayat Eslaminia, formerly a high-ranking Iranian official, to turn over his assets (estimated in the millions) to Reza, who would split it with the BBC. After careful planning, Hunt, Reza, and three other BBC members allegedly kidnapped the elder Eslaminia on July 30, 1984. They crammed him into a trunk, which they loaded into their car. Then they headed for a Los Angeles hideout where they planned to torture the elder Eslaminia in order to gain control of his money. However, the kidnapping victim suffocated in the trunk en route. The killers dumped the dead man's body into a steep canyon. Later, after Hunt and the others told the BBC membership about the murders, some worried members contacted the police, dispelling earlier conjecture that the elder Eslaminia had fallen victim to Iranian assassins. Police were directed to the dumping spot where Eslaminia's bones were found and identified.

After the arrests of the guilty parties, Joe Hunt was tried and found guilty of first-degree murder in the death of Levin, whose body was never recovered. Hunt received a life sentence in June 1987. In 1988, Reza Eslaminia was sentenced to life, with no possibility of parole, for the murder of Hedayat Eslaminia. Pittman's trial for the Levin slaying was pending as of the last report, as was Hunt's for the Eslaminia murder. One BBC member was given immunity and placed under the witness protection program for testifying against those charged with the murders.

LAWRENCE BITTAKER AND ROY NORRIS

THEY VOWED THEIR KILLING SPREE WOULD NOT END UNTIL THEY HAD RAPED AND KILLED A GIRL OF EACH AGE FROM 13 TO 19.

The trial of Lawrence Bittaker made history as the first felony trial in the state of California to allow television cameras. But the family and friends of the five teenage girls who were viciously savaged by Bittaker and cohort Roy Norris will remember it as the place where justice was served.

The random killings involved rape, torture, and mutilation in what Norris said was a plot to kill for fun that they cooked up while in prison. While convicted of only five slayings, police believed the November 1979 arrests could clear up the mystery behind as many as 30 to 40 missing persons cases.

Bittaker and Norris met in a California prison in 1978. Bittaker was serving time for assault with a deadly weapon and Norris for rape. While still behind bars, the two passed the time plotting a killing spree that, if successful, would not end until one girl of each age between 13 and 19 had been raped and killed.

Bittaker, paroled in November 1978, was awaiting Norris's 1979 release. He had already purchased a van he named "Murder Mack," which they would later use as death central.

By June 24, 1979, just nine days after Norris was released, teenage girls started to disappear. The first girl that police know about was 16-year-old Linda Schaeffer, who was last seen at a church function.

Joy Hall, age 18, disappeared about two weeks later. Two other girls disappeared two months afterward while hitchhiking near Redondo Beach. They were later identified as Jacqueline Lamp, 13, and Jackie Gilliam, 15.

The final victim actually attributed by a court to Bittaker and Norris was Shirley Ledford, 16, who vanished on Halloween. Unlike the others, she was found the next morning, in the residential area of Tijunga. Her body gave police the first indication of exactly how grisly and sadistic these murderers were. Her face and breasts were mutilated, her arms slashed, and her body covered with bruises.

Police arrested Bittaker and Norris November 20 in connection with a rape in Hermosa Beach. The victim told police she was sprayed with Mace and thrown into a silver van. She was raped but managed to escape. She did not identify either suspect, but both were held on parole violations and for drug possession.

While Bittaker and Norris were in police custody, investigators searching the house and motel where the two had lived found more than 500 photographs of teenage girls. At least 19 of the photos were of girls reported missing, but 60 of the others were reported alive and well. Confiscated from the van was a grisly souvenir—an audiotape containing a live recording of the murder of Lamp.

Norris confessed to the murders and told police how they cruised the streets offering girls rides, marijuana, and modeling jobs. He also told how they forced their victims into the van and drove them to isolated areas. On February 9, 1980, police uncovered the graves of Lamp and Gilliam and found an ice pick still sticking out of Gilliam's skull.

Norris made a deal with prosecutors to confess and testify against Bittaker in exchange for a lighter sentence. He was convicted of the five slayings and given 45 years to life with the possibility of parole after 30 years. Bittaker bitterly fought his murder rap and the ruling allowing cameras in the court. But the judge let the cameras roll as Norris told the gruesome story. Bittaker was sentenced to death, but just in case, the judge added a sentence of 199 years and four months to take effect in the event his sentence is ever commuted.

THE BOSTON STRANGLER
ALBERT DeSALVO

HE RAPED HER AT KNIFE-POINT, STRANGLED HER WITH HIS HANDS, AND PROCEEDED TO "DECORATE" HER BODY FOR THE POLICE, COMPLETE WITH A NEW YEAR'S CARD PLACED BETWEEN HER TOES.

One of the most infamous serial killers in American history, Albert DeSalvo descended into his own private hell in the summer of 1962 and emerged as the Boston Strangler. His reign of terror began on June 14 with the gruesome strangulation of his first victim, Mrs. Anna Slesers, a 55-year-old divorced seamstress. Slesers, found nude on the floor outside her bathroom, was discovered by her son. Her housecoat had been thrown open, and she had been strangled with its cord. About two weeks later, 85-year-old Mary Mullen was found dead, though her death was not attributed to the same perpetrator at that time. Just a few days later, two elderly victims were discovered strangled in nearby Brighton and Lynn townships.

Mrs. Nina Nichols, a retired therapist who was 68 years old, and Miss Helen Blake, a 65-year-old registered nurse, had both been choked to death with nylon stockings. Nichols had been on the telephone when the doorbell rang. Eerily, the person on the other end of the line heard the bell when it chimed. Nichols excused herself, saying she would call right back, but she never did.

It was obvious that a grim pattern was forming in which older women—mothers, aunts, grandmothers—were meeting violent, sexually motivated deaths. Eleven days later, a 60-year-old widow, Mrs. Margaret Davis, was found strangled, this time by hand. The murderer seemed to want to get closer to his victims, more familiar.

When 75-year-old Mrs. Ida Irga—a sweet little old lady who lived alone—turned up dead on August 19, Bostonians began to panic. Mrs. Irga had been sexually assaulted and left propped up in a lewd display, as if in preparation for discovery. Details of the assault were kept secret to aid in identifying the killer, but that simply made the rumor mill churn more wildly. About ten days later, Miss Jane Sullivan, another nurse in her sixties, was found dead in Dorchester. Evidence showed that Miss Sullivan, a big woman, put up a valiant fight, but to no avail. She had been strangled with a nylon stocking, and her death had occurred several days before she was found.

At this point, the pattern seemed to gel. The killer was seeking highly vulnerable victims. Senior citizens braced themselves. Neighbors of elderly women kept a watchful vigil. After he remained inactive for over three months, the Strangler struck again on December 5, 1962. Confounding everyone, he did not pick an elderly woman. He chose Sophie Clark, a 21-year-old student who had two roommates. Boston's reputation as a college town put a staggering number of young women open to attack. Sophie Clark could not have been more different from the previous victims. She was young, outgoing, active, and African-American. Still, she was attending a school of medical technology and lived only two blocks from the first victim. Before the year was out, the Boston Strangler struck again, murdering Patricia Bissette, a 23-year-old secretary, on December 30.

A little over two months into the new year, the Strangler struck again, savagely killing Mary Brown, age 69, on March 9, 1963. Then came the vicious murder of 23-year-old Beverly Samans on May 6, 1963. The death of Evelyn Corbin, a vivacious divorcée of 58, was shocking for its audacity. She was assaulted after returning from breakfast at her neighbor's down the hallway. The Strangler was waiting in Corbin's apartment when she arrived. By the time this same neighbor called less than an hour later, the Strangler had sexually abused and murdered Corbin. The next murder was even more shocking for its sense of timing. The day after the assassination of President John F. Kennedy, who was Boston's famous son, 23-year-old Joann Graff became another victim on November 23, 1963.

The killer's last murder was his most outrageous. Once again, he chose a college student, 19-year-old Mary Sullivan. On January 4, 1964, he broke into the apartment where she lived with two roommates. He raped her at knife-point, strangled her with his hands, and proceeded to "decorate" her body for the police, complete with a New Year's card placed between her toes. The details were hard to keep out of the press, no matter how cryptic the wording. The death of pretty, young Mary Sullivan was the last straw. The state of Massachusetts turned all the cases over to the state attorney general's office. Eventually, more than 2,600 law enforcement agents became involved.

The murders had enough similarities to suggest a single killer. All the victims were women who were strangled—some by hand, most by nylon stockings. Each was attacked while alone in her apartment. All were left in a nude state and were sexually violated. There was no pattern to the sexual activity. Although the first victim had not been raped, evidence suggested that the killer had engaged in some type of solo sexual activity. The

Strangler had raped and desecrated the bodies of Nina Nichols and Helen Blake. So the theory of a sadistic, woman-hating killer seemed to be valid.

The police had never found any evidence that would lead to a description of the killer. No one ever seemed to notice him. The lack of signs of forced entry was particularly disturbing because of all the media hysteria and official warnings to single women. The police began to resort to unusual sources for help, employing various clairvoyants and ESP sensitives. The most famous of these was Peter Hurkos. His description of the Strangler led the police to arrest a mentally disturbed shoe salesman, who turned out to have nothing to do with the stranglings.

The police also turned to psychiatrists for help. A task force was put together that included autopsy examiners, gynecologists, and therapists specializing in treating sex criminals. They were ordered to create a character/personality sketch. They found that the killer had a consuming rage toward women and that he suffered from an Oedipus complex. These "experts" also deduced that the Strangler was impotent and that he violently hated all women.

In September 1964, nine months after the last strangling, a man attacked a young married coed in her apartment. He forced her onto her bed, raped her, and immediately left. Using police mug shots, the woman identified Albert DeSalvo as her assailant.

DeSalvo had previously spent 11 months in jail for breaking and entering. He had been released in April 1962, just three months before Anna Slesers was killed. DeSalvo had been known as "the Measuring Man." He approached young women in their homes and offered them a chance to apply for high-paying modeling jobs. All they had to do was allow Mr. DeSalvo to take their physical measurements. Strange as this sounds, he was quite successful at it. Since this scheme would not go over with his elderly strangling victims, DeSalvo apparently posed as a repairman.

When DeSalvo was arrested for the September 1964 rape of the young married coed, he was sent to Bridgewater State Hospital. DeSalvo began to boast to other inmates. One inmate took him seriously and informed DeSalvo's lawyer, the young F. Lee Bailey. To test DeSalvo's veracity, Bailey obtained a list of confidential questions. When satisfied of DeSalvo's guilt, Bailey informed the police that his client was the Boston Strangler. Since the police had no concrete evidence, they were forced to agree to Bailey's terms. The police could not use the confessions against DeSalvo. They gave up the right to prosecute him for the murders in exchange for the certainty that the Boston Strangler was off the streets.

However, the police and psychiatrists just couldn't accept that DeSalvo was the real Boston Strangler. He turned out to be more deviant than anyone imagined. The police had been looking for a perverted genius—figuring that only a master criminal could elude them. And yet he turned out to be a very ordinary man. This dull, uneducated, ordinary man eluded capture simply because there was no rhyme nor reason to his attacks. Albert DeSalvo himself never knew when he would strike until the urge came over him.

DeSalvo was a married man with two children. He was deeply devoted to his wife, and most of his post-arrest efforts were aimed at sheltering her. He did not hate his mother; he simply pitied her for the abuse she had received from his father. DeSalvo offered as his sole motive an absolutely consuming sexual appetite. He had sex with his wife about five times a day (more on weekends) and sought outside relations to supplement these urges. DeSalvo reckoned that he had raped more than 2,000 women in his lifetime. The police confirmed at least 300 in the Boston/New England area. He was found to have raped three different women in separate cities in a three-hour span.

Albert DeSalvo was sentenced to life imprisonment for rape, but never stood trial for any of the murders. DeSalvo was stabbed to death in prison in 1973, allegedly over a drug deal.

IAN BRADY AND MYRA HINDLEY

HARDENED POLICE OFFICERS THOUGHT THEY HAD SEEN AND HEARD EVERYTHING UNTIL THEY HEARD THE TAPE OF A MURDER IN PROGRESS.

The desolate English moors—large expanses of rolling, infertile land covered with stunted vegetation—were the setting for a series of killings by two of the most vicious murderers who ever lived. The quiet town of Hattersley, England, surrounded by moors, was the home of Ian Brady, 28, and Myra Hindley, 23. The couple lived together in Hindley's grandmother's house.

No one seemed to know the couple well, but those people who were aware of them found little out of the ordinary. Only one other couple seemed friendly with them—Hindley's sister, Maureen Smith, and her husband David.

On the night of October 6, 1965, Myra Hindley left her sister's house to go home, accompanied by her brother-in-law David Smith. They went into Hindley's kitchen for a glass of wine. Later, David described what happened: "All of a sudden I heard a very loud scream, very loud. Just before it died out another one followed it. Then Myra shouted out, 'Come help him!' I didn't know what was coming. I just ran out of the kitchen and into the living room, and I just froze and stopped dead. My first thought was that Ian had hold of a life-size doll and was just waving it about. Then it dawned on me that it was not a rag doll."

The "doll" was actually Edward Evans, 17. Brady struck him repeatedly with an ax—the autopsy showed 14 times. To make the hideous deed certain, Brady strangled his victim.

The murder had been a "demonstration" for David Smith. He had a long juvenile record of violence and drank heavily. To Brady and Hindley, David seemed a perfect candidate to recruit to help them in their crimes. David, in shock, helped the couple clean up the mess and prepare the body for burial. As they swabbed the blood from the walls and floor, Brady made sick jokes about the victim being a bleeder, a deadweight, and a brainy swine. When David Smith got home, he became very sick and vomited for hours. He told his wife what had happened, and at 6 A.M., they went to the police.

Thus was uncovered one of the ghastliest series of child murders in England's history. The graves of two missing children, Lesley Ann Downey, 10, and John Kilbride, 12, were found. Brady and Hindley were suspected in at least 11 other murders or disappearances. Brady and Hindley denied any guilt in the hideous crimes, but Brady helped convict himself by taking a picture of Myra on the moors. She was looking down at a disturbed patch of dirt. Officers located the spot and dug up the body of John Kilbride.

Lesley Ann Downey, who had been missing for ten months, had been subjected to unspeakable horrors worse than her brutal death. The child had been stripped, photographed in pornographic poses, and subjected to sexual abuse. During her torment, the callous pair had made a recording of her screams and pleas. Brady and Hindley then added seasonal Christmas music to the tape. Police found the tape recording of the last hours of her brief life. Hardened police officers—who thought they had seen and heard everything—said the tape of the murder in progress carried the most heartbreaking sounds they had ever heard.

During the trial, Hindley sat without expression. She even listened to the tape of Lesley crying and begging for her life without any sign of remorse, though several jurors and spectators wept openly. Brady was more emotional. When Myra Hindley told the jury that the ghastly murders were totally Brady's scheme, he burst into obscenities. Brady and Hindley were both found guilty and sentenced to life in prison.

THEODORE "TED" BUNDY

PERSONABLE AND ATTRACTIVE, BUNDY PLAYED UPON THE SYMPATHY OF WOMEN TO ENTRAP THEM.

Intelligent, good-looking, and amusing, Ted Bundy seemed nothing like a serial killer. Although he was illegitimate and for years his mother led him to believe she was his older sister, his childhood was otherwise uneventful. People were not sure, when Bundy appeared in a Utah courtroom in 1975, whether he was really a vicious murderer or just a case of mistaken identity.

Bundy's first victim is believed to be Sharon Clarke of Seattle, Washington. In January 1974, the young woman was beaten with a metal rod while she was asleep. Clarke survived the assault. Four weeks later, Lynda Ann Healy, a University of Washington student, vanished from her room in a group house. The other residents of the house heard no sounds of a struggle that night, but her bedsheets were found bloodstained. Within five months, five other coeds at schools in Washington and northern Oregon had also disappeared.

The last was Georgann Hawkins, who was seen

by several students on the night of June 11, 1974. She had been walking down a well-lit alley behind fraternity and sorority houses on the University of Washington campus. Hawkins vanished only a few yards from the back doorstep of her sorority house. Her fate remains a mystery.

On July 14, 1974, two young women vanished from Lake Sammanish Park in Washington. One, Janice Ott, was seen accompanying a handsome young man to his Volkswagen. The man had his arm in a sling and called himself "Ted."

The disappearances ceased in the Seattle area. However, that fall, the skeletal remains of the missing women were found in wilderness graves throughout the region. By that time the disappearances had shifted to Salt Lake City, where Bundy had enrolled in law school. Soon the crimes embraced neighboring Colorado.

Bundy was already being suspected of these crimes. A former girlfriend of his from Seattle, Liz Kendall, had informed police it was possible that Bundy might be the "Ted" they were looking for. But Bundy was just one of more than 2,000 suspects until, on August 16, 1975, an off-duty patrolman in Salt Lake City arrested Bundy after he operated his Volkswagen in a suspicious manner. In the car, the patrolman found a ski mask, an ice pick, a crowbar, and other paraphernalia that contradicted Bundy's law-student posture.

Bundy was then identified by Carol DaRonch as the man who had tried to abduct her in November 1974. After being convicted of kidnapping DaRonch, he was extradited to Colorado to stand trial for the murder of Caryn Campbell. Bundy escaped twice during the pretrial hearings. His second attempt left him free for nearly two months. Before he was recaptured, he had slain Kimberley Leach, a junior high school student, and Lisa Levy and Margaret Bowman, sorority sisters at Florida State University in Tallahassee. On July 23, 1979, Bundy was convicted of the murders largely because his teeth matched the bite marks left on Lisa Levy's buttocks.

Although sentenced to be executed, Bundy maintained his innocence. Carole Ann Boone, one of many who believed Bundy, married him while he was on death row. To the embarrassment of Florida prison officials, she conceived a child with him during one of her routine visits.

Ted Bundy differed from most sex killers in that he was personable and attractive. The frenzy that caused him to beat his victims unconscious and then rape and kill them was never explained. Bundy asked his accusers why he would rape and kill women when he had all he could want. On January 24, 1989, Ted Bundy went to the electric chair with his question still unanswered.

ROBERT CHAMBERS

HIS PREPPIE LIFESTYLE EVENTUALLY LED TO ALCO-HOL, DRUGS, AND KILLING.

Robert Chambers was born in Queens, New York, in the 1960s. His mother, Phyllis, doted on him, spoiling him and excusing his faults. She also had social ambitions, and to meet the "right" people, she enrolled Robert in the "best" schools. Phyllis became involved at school and did charity work.

Phyllis spoiled her son, but she also demanded a great deal of him. She pushed her son to be an altar boy and to join the Knickerbocker Greys, an after-school military drill group nicknamed the "Social Register's Private Little Army."

Despite these social advantages, Chambers fell into bad ways. At an early age, he began using drugs. He was expelled from one school, and then another. He began hanging out with some of his prep-school buddies, some of whom also were into drugs. They were habitués at a bar called Dorrian's Red Hand, drinking until late at night. Sleeping around was a common practice. This lifestyle was expensive, but Chambers was able to finance it by stealing from the homes of his wealthier friends.

Jennifer Levin was part of this social circle. She fell for the 19-year-old Chambers—a handsome, daring bad boy. The pair dated a few times. Although she was very interested in him, he seemed indifferent. On August 26, 1986, Levin and Chambers left Dorrian's Red Hand together about 4:30 A.M.

Later that morning, Levin's body was found in Central Park with her clothes bunched around her waist. Eighteen hours later, Chambers confessed to killing her; he claimed it was an accident. They had gone to Central Park, where Levin's sexual advances were not welcomed by Chambers. Trying to stop her, Chambers said, he flipped her over his head, accidentally killing her.

A combination of poor police investigative work and an experienced defense lawyer undermined the prosecution's case. The jury deliberated for days without reaching a verdict. Finally, a plea bargain was worked out. Chambers pleaded guilty to manslaughter, but he had to admit in court that he had "intended to cause serious physical injury to Jennifer." Chambers was sentenced to five to 15 years in prison; he will be eligible for parole in 1993.

MARK DAVID CHAPMAN

A LOSER'S LIFE SPIRALED DOWNWARD, UNTIL MARK DAVID CHAPMAN "SUCCEEDED" AT ONE THING——THE KILLING OF JOHN LENNON.

Although Mark David Chapman—born in 1955 in Fort Worth, Texas—appeared to have a normal childhood, much of it was difficult and unhappy. In grade school, the other children teased and tormented him. An inferiority complex that would be a hallmark of his adult life began to develop. Chapman was timid and afraid to fight back at school. Instead, he imagined a fantasy world in which "little people" lived in the walls of his room and were ruled by Chapman.

Unable to cope with his inadequacies as he grew into adolescence, Chapman turned to drugs. As a freshman in high school, he began sniffing glue, smoking marijuana, and snorting cocaine. Less frequently he took heroin, LSD, methamphetamines, and barbiturates. After he burned himself out, Chapman became a religious fanatic.

By the time he reached adulthood, Chapman

seemed doomed to failure at every turn. He did poorly at junior college and dropped out, had an unstable marriage, and couldn't seem to hold a job. Chapman became physically abusive to those closest to him, and he eventually attempted suicide.

Feeling shut out and betrayed by nearly everyone connected to him, Chapman traveled to New York in December 1980. He was determined to succeed at something, however grim. He finally decided he would kill former Beatle John Lennon, whom he perceived as "phony and insincere," in order to become well known.

On December 8, 1980, Chapman went to the Dakota apartment building at 72nd Street and Central Park West where Lennon and his wife, Yoko Ono, lived. Chapman was packing a Charter Arms .38, which he had bought only two days earlier, concealed in the pocket of his coat.

Pacing beneath the Dakota's archway, Chapman spotted the singer-songwriter leaving the building early in the day and obtained Lennon's autograph. Unable to carry out his plan of murder at that time, Chapman went back to his hotel room and prayed to Satan for the strength that he needed to shoot John Lennon.

Then, more determined than ever and carrying his highly cherished copy of J. D. Salinger's *The Catcher in the Rye*, Chapman returned to the Dakota later that afternoon and began his vigil anew.

Appearing to be just another autograph hound, Chapman waited all day for Lennon to return. Finally, at about 10:50 P.M., he saw Lennon and Yoko pull up in front of the apartment building in their limousine.

Yoko climbed out of the car first and was about 40 feet ahead of Lennon when he exited the vehicle. As Lennon approached the Dakota's archway, he looked directly at Chapman. But by then it was too late. Chapman had taken the .38 out of his coat pocket and began firing in rapid succession. When it was over, five shots had been fired.

As John Lennon crumbled to the sidewalk in front of his home and his horrified wife, Chapman's only thoughts were, "The bullets are working." At a tremendous cost to the world, not to mention Lennon's family and friends, Mark David Chapman had finally found success. After pleading guilty to murder, Chapman was sentenced to a life term at the Attica prison in upstate New York.

JOHN REGINALD CHRISTIE

LURKING BENEATH THE CLOAK OF MEEKNESS WAS A BEAST WHOSE SEXUAL GRATIFICATION CAME IN THE FORM OF FEMALE CORPSES.

For John Reginald Christie, sex and murder went hand in hand—and he wasn't picky about which came first. In the span of 13 years, he brutally murdered and raped eight women, including his wife.

On the surface, Christie appeared to be a shy, harmless man. But lurking beneath the cloak of meekness was a beast whose sexual gratification came in the form of female corpses. Christie's sexual inadequacy could find its release only in violent sex leading to murder.

In most cases, Christie strangled his victim to death and then had sex with the dead body. Sometimes, however, he raped the woman first, and the murder came as the unintended climax of the violent assault. If the victim survived the rape, Christie murdered her afterward to cover his tracks.

On November 30, 1949, Timothy Evans,

Christie's neighbor, came home and discovered that his wife and 14-month-old daughter had been strangled to death. Panicked, Evans fled London. A few days later, he walked into a police station in Wales and told the authorities about his wife and child. After an investigation, Evans was charged and tried for the murders.

Evans confessed to the murders during his trial, but he also blamed his neighbor, John Christie, for the deaths. The jury found Evans guilty, and he was hanged in 1950. Although some observers felt that Evans did kill his daughter, and perhaps his wife, others believed that Christie had terrified Evans into confessing to crimes that Christie himself had committed.

In December 1952, Christie's wife disappeared. During the next two months, Christie picked up and killed two prostitutes.

On March 24, 1953, another tenant in Christie's building broke down a wall while renovating an apartment and found the decomposed bodies of three women. The authorities soon arrived, and when they dug up Christie's garden, more victims were uncovered. Mrs. Christie was discovered under the floorboards.

John Christie was arrested and tried. To convince the jurors he was insane, Christie divulged his diseased sexual inclinations. His insanity plea rejected, Christie was hanged on July 15, 1953.

ALTON COLEMAN AND
DEBRA BROWN

OVER A SEVEN-WEEK PERIOD, COLEMAN AND BROWN
TRAVELED THROUGH SIX STATES, REPEATEDLY COM-
MITTING ROBBERY, ASSAULT, KIDNAPPING, RAPE,
AND MURDER.

On May 29, 1984, nine-year-old Vernita Wheat of
Kenosha, Wisconsin, convinced her mother to let
her take a trip with Robert Knight, a new acquaintance of the family, and his girlfriend. The three
were to go to Waukegan, Illinois, to pick up a
stereo. When they had not returned the next day,
Vernita's mother notified police, who determined
that Knight was actually Alton Coleman and the
girlfriend was Debra Brown. Three weeks later,
Vernita's body was found in an abandoned
Waukegan warehouse; she had been strangled.

The young girl's death marked the beginning of
a brutal Midwestern crime spree that took the
efforts of the FBI and 45 local police departments to
end. Over a seven-week period, Coleman and

Brown would travel seemingly at will through six states, repeatedly committing robbery, assault, kidnapping, rape, and murder. Authorities knew the criminals' identities and had complete descriptions and fingerprint records of them, but the couple somehow managed to stay at least a few steps ahead of capture.

The next crime occurred in Gary, Indiana, on June 18. Seven-year-old Tameka Turks and her nine-year-old aunt were abducted, raped, and beaten; Tameka was murdered, but her aunt was able to escape. The next day, Donna Williams, 25, was reported missing; police determined that she had recently been in contact with Coleman and Brown. Her body was found in Detroit nearly three weeks later. Over the next 18 days, the couple were identified as the assailants in several robberies and beatings in Michigan and Ohio.

On July 7, they spent the night in the home of Virginia Temple of Toledo. They had been introduced to Temple by a local minister that the couple had befriended. When they left the house the next morning, Temple and her ten-year-old daughter Rachelle were dead; the young girl had been raped.

In the weeks that followed, the count of victims continued to rise. In Cincinnati, a teenage girl was abducted, stabbed repeatedly, and shot twice in the head. A suburban woman was bludgeoned to death and her husband was severely beaten. A man from Kentucky was kidnapped and his car was stolen, but he was released unharmed. An elderly minister and his wife in Dayton, Ohio, were beaten and their car was stolen. Finally, a 77-year-old Zionsville, Indiana, man was abducted and murdered; he had been stabbed numerous times and shot four times in the head.

In the end, Coleman and Brown were captured in Evanston, Illinois, a suburb of Chicago, on July 20. Police had been concentrating the search in that area, but a tip led to the arrest; a high school acquaintance of Coleman's recognized him as he walked down the street in Evanston. The couple were arrested a short time later as they sat in the bleachers near a basketball court in a park. Although both were armed, they offered no resistance.

Bond for Coleman was set at $25 million cash. "This nation has been under a siege," said U.S. Magistrate Carl Sussman in setting bond. "This nation has been under a reign of terror, not knowing when the next victim was going to be taken. I am going to make sure no other victim will be the subject of this man." Brown was later arraigned, and her bond was set at $20 million cash.

The first of several trials then began. The couple first faced charges in Cincinnati for two murders. Tried separately, both were convicted of the murders and sentenced to death. They were then tried in Indiana, where they received death sentences for the murder of Tameka Turks. In addition, Coleman received a 100-year sentence for the attempted murder of Turks' 9-year-old aunt and two consecutive 40-year sentences for kidnapping and child molesting. Illinois also tried Coleman and imposed a third death sentence on him.

Although authorities had ample evidence against them in many other crimes, including the murders of the mother and daughter from Toledo and the elderly man from Indiana, officials did not prosecute the couple in those cases, perhaps figuring that with death sentences in three states for Coleman and two states for Brown, their deaths were certain.

ADOLFO DE JESUS CONSTANZO

THE BRAIN, HEART, AND OTHER ORGANS OF SOME VICTIMS HAD BEEN REMOVED. ONE SUSPECT EVEN WORE THE SPINAL CORD OF ONE VICTIM AS A NECKLACE.

Police ended a nine-month ritualistic killing spree on April 11, 1989, when they found shallow graves of brutalized victims on a ranch near Matamoros, Mexico. But their investigation led to an even more grisly discovery—a cauldron filled with animal blood. Floating in the blood were the head of a goat, chicken feet, a turtle, herbs, a horseshoe—even the charred remains of a human brain. These gruesome items were thought to be part of a ritual ceremony.

Five drug smugglers, including at least one American, were immediately arrested. They explained that they believed human sacrifice could protect them from police and bullets and even help them make more money.

A nationwide hunt followed for 27-year-old drug kingpin Adolfo de Jesus Constanzo, a Cuban

American also known as El Padrino or the Godfather, and his 24-year-old girlfriend, Sara Maria Aldrete, also known as the Witch.

Members of the ring told police Constanzo masterminded a drug-smuggling operation that shipped more than 2,000 pounds of marijuana across the border every week. They also said Constanzo introduced them to the world of black magic and human sacrifice as a method of shielding their operation.

Experts theorized Constanzo created his own hybrid of several occults, taking practices from Santeria, a Caribbean voodoo religious cult; Bruja, a belief in witchcraft dating back to 16th century Aztec Indians; and Satanism. A connection was also possible to a 1987 film, *The Believers*, which included child sacrifices, cults, and Santeria.

The victims included a 14-year-old boy and a 21-year-old University of Texas pre-med student, Mark Kilroy, the first body to be identified. Police said most of the victims had died of either a machete or hammer blow. All had been mutilated. Some had been boiled alive. The brain, heart, and other organs of some victims had been removed. One suspect even wore the spinal cord of one victim as a necklace.

News of the grisly murders started a run on the community of Matamoros. Relatives of missing young men gathered to find out if their loved ones had fallen victim to the sadistic killings. The Kilroy family heard the horrible tale of how Mark, who was on spring break in Matamoros, had been lured away from his friends on a crowded street at about 2 A.M. on March 14. At first authorities said he had been picked at random, but later authorities learned through confessions that Kilroy had been "chosen" because he resembled Constanzo. After Kilroy's death, the group had opened his head to steal his brain and give Constanzo his intelligence, a Mexican police chief said.

Constanzo lived in Mexico City, had a home and family in Miami, and maintained a mailing address in Brownsville, Texas, just across the border from Matamoros. He had no record of prior arrest, but others involved told police he was the ringleader and mastermind of the cult. He was also reported to be the one who convinced the crew that human sacrifices could shield them from harm.

Sara Maria Aldrete was a college student by day, but off campus she was Constanzo's girlfriend and was allegedly also involved in gruesome Satanic activity. Aldrete was well known at Texas Southmost College in Brownsville; she was a member of the school's *Who's Who* and the winner of several academic awards. But at her home in Matamoros, police found a Satanic-style altar, blood-spattered children's clothes, and pictures of three children.

Police were alerted as far away as Illinois, where the two had friends in the Chicago area. While the hunt for the pair was on, events at the ranch continued to unfold. Two more bodies found on a nearby farm were linked to the cult, bringing the death total to 15. However, these were believed to be revenge killings stemming from drug deals rather than ritualistic mutilations.

Police finally caught up with the Satanic fugitives less than a month later in Mexico City. Aldrete was captured and indicted, but Constanzo was killed in a death pact. He ordered one of his men to kill him.

KEVIN COOPER

COOPER USED A HATCHET, A KNIFE, AND PERHAPS A SCREWDRIVER OR ICE PICK TO TAKE THE LIVES OF HIS VICTIMS.

A man who escaped from a Pennsylvania mental hospital, where he was confined because he was unfit to stand trial on a burglary charge, committed the brutal ax murder of a California family.

Kevin Cooper walked away from Pennsylvania's Mayview State Hospital near Pittsburgh in October 1982. Hours later, a 17-year-old girl was abducted from her home and raped by Cooper, a screwdriver used as the weapon of threat.

Using the identification of Mayview patient David Trautman, Cooper traveled to California. He was arrested by Los Angeles police in January 1983 on burglary charges and was sentenced to four years at the California Institute for Men in Chino, California. California officials believed him to be David Trautman. Because he was serving a burglary sentence, Cooper was placed in the minimum security section of the Chino prison, where only an eight-foot chain-link fence separated him from the rest of society. Less than 24 hours later, he hopped the fence and started on a path that would lead to brutality and violence.

Three days later, on June 5, Cooper met the Ryen family. The Ryens—father Douglas, mother Peggy, 10-year-old Jessica, and 8-year-old Joshua—lived about five miles from the prison on a remote hill-top. An 11-year-old family friend, Chris Hughes, was sleeping over at the Ryens's that night.

When Cooper left the Ryen home in the couple's white station wagon, the blood-spattered ranch house held the brutally stabbed bodies of Douglas, Peggy, Jessica, and Chris Hughes. Eight-year-old Joshua, his neck severely slashed, was barely cling-ing to life when the grisly scene was discovered by Chris's father, William Hughes, who had come to pick up his son. Cooper's tools had been a hatchet, a knife, and perhaps a screwdriver or ice pick.

Police issued an arrest warrant for Cooper just four days later, but he eluded capture for two months. He left the Ryens's car near Long Beach and made his way to Ensenada. There he met 35-year-old Owen Handy of Humboldt County.

Handy, his wife, and their five-year-old daugh-ter were living on a 32-foot sailboat anchored in Pelican Cove near the east end of Santa Cruz Island, about 25 miles from the Santa Barbara shore. They took Cooper on as a deckhand.

Anchored about 50 yards from the Handys' boat was that of another couple. The couple invited the Handys and Cooper over for a Friday night fish fry. Later that evening, Cooper returned to the couple's boat and raped the woman, threatening her with a knife, while her husband slept. When he returned to the Handys' boat, the victim contacted police.

When the Coast Guard and sheriff's deputies arrived, Cooper had already swum out to a small dinghy and was making his way to dry land. When he was apprehended by deputies, he was only 200 yards from shore. Although he told police upon his arrest his name was Angel Jackson, fingerprints identified him as Cooper. Handy told police he was unaware that Cooper was being sought for murder, and so was not charged.

DEAN CORLL, WAYNE HENLEY, AND DAVID BROOKS

HENLEY AND BROOKS WOULD LURE THE VICTIMS—ONE AS YOUNG AS NINE—TO CORLL'S APARTMENT FOR PAINT-SNIFFING ORGIES THAT ULTIMATELY ENDED IN DEATH.

Appearances can be deceiving. The neighbors of 33-year-old Dean Corll in a suburb of Houston thought him a nice man, always giving the boys treats from his candy store.

But Corll, 17-year-old Elmer Wayne Henley, and 18-year-old David Owen Brooks became linked to a shocking series of homosexual murders. When the total number of victims reached 27 dead boys, the police stopped counting.

Corll's homosexual tendencies first surfaced in 1964 while serving in the Army. After he returned to the Heights neighborhood in Houston, Corll started making friends with young boys. In 1969, Corll met Brooks and Henley the same way he met other neighborhood boys: He enticed them with free candy. But the candy was just a start. Corll was soon hosting glue-sniffing and paint-sniffing parties at his suburban apartment in Pasadena.

Brooks first learned of Corll's sadistic streak in 1970. Brooks happened into Corll's apartment to find him naked with two nude boys strapped to a homemade torture rack. Soon after buying Brooks's silence with the gift of a car, Corll enlisted both Brooks and Henley as agents to find victims at a price of $200 per head.

Brooks later told police that from mid-1970 through August 1973, the three of them shared in the joy of killing. Henley and Brooks would lure the victims—one as young as nine—to Corll's apartment for paint-sniffing orgies that ultimately ended in death. Some murders occurred two at a time. At least two sets of brothers are believed to have fallen victim to the homosexual candy man.

Most of the victims disappeared from the Heights neighborhood, a lower-class area where as many as 180 juveniles a year were reported to Houston police as missing. On May 29, 1971, the Hilligiest family reported their son missing, but the police classified most of these cases as runaways. Selma Winkle—whose own 16-year-old son had vanished with the Hilligiest boy—couldn't understand how the police could call the boys runaways. She told police that they had nothing on but their bathing suits and only 80 cents between them.

The Hilligiests spent what little available money they had on a private detective. They put flyers out on the street with a photo of their young son and even sought the help of a psychic. Among the little solace they found was the concern of Henley; he always asked about the search and even volunteered to pass out posters. But it wasn't until Henley himself called the police August 8, 1973, that the Hilligiests finally learned the truth.

Henley told police he took a friend to one of Corll's paint-sniffing orgies, but it was a female friend. Corll was outraged and drew a gun. Henley took the gun during the ensuing struggle and put six slugs in Corll's back and shoulder; Henley told police he shot in self-defense.

Henley then gave police a guided tour of the trio's burial grounds. Under a rented boat shed in southwest Houston, police uncovered 17 bodies. Another four graves were found at Lake Sam Rayburn and six more on the beach at Highland Island. Henley claimed he knew of four more burial sites, and a book published later suggested others were buried around the candy shop.

Henley was convicted of multiple murders in August 1974 and sentenced to life in prison, as was Brooks in March 1975. Henley's conviction was later overturned, but he was convicted again in June 1979, receiving the same fate.

JUAN CORONA

THE BODIES OF 25 MEN WERE FOUND. SOME WERE NAKED. THE TROUSERS OF SOME HAD BEEN LEFT PULLED AROUND THE VICTIMS' ANKLES.

Peaches are a major crop in the lush farming region around Yuba City, California, but in 1971, the bountiful orchards yielded a harvest of murder.

The crop of corpses was discovered after a farmer noticed a large hole on his land that, later on the same day, had mysteriously been filled. On that day, May 19, 1971, authorities unearthed the corpse of a transient named Kenneth Whitacre. He had been stabbed to death and his head had been mutilated by a sharp object (later determined to be a machete). Investigators found gay literature in Whitacre's pocket and physical evidence of homosexual intercourse.

Four days later, a tractor driver spotted what looked like a grave on another ranch near Yuba City. Officers unearthed the mutilated body of an elderly man. By June 4, the bodies of 25 men ranging from age 40 to 68 had been found. Some corpses were naked; others partially clothed. The trousers of some had been left pulled around the victims' ankles. All of the bodies had been mutilated with a machete and bore evidence of homosexual encounters.

Found in two graves were bank deposit slips bearing the name Juan Corona. The 38-year-old Corona, a contractor supplying workers for seasonal fruit picking, had come from Mexico in the 1950s as a migrant laborer. Officers searched Corona's house and found bloodstained clothing and weapons, including a machete.

Corona, a schizophrenic, may have been involved in a 1970 Marysville, California, incident in which a severely beaten young Mexican man was discovered, alive, in the men's room of a cafe owned by Corona's homosexual half-brother, Natividad. The victim's head wounds were similar to those discovered on the 25 bodies unearthed in 1971.

Natividad had fled to Mexico after the young man recovered and successfully sued Natividad for assault. Juan remained in the United States and lived a seemingly normal life with a wife, children, and ordinary sexual tendencies.

At Corona's trial, the defense suggested that there were two killers and that neither of them was Corona. Nevertheless, the jury convicted Corona and sentenced him to 25 consecutive life sentences.

HARVEY CRIPPEN

IN ENGLAND, THE NAME OF THE QUASI-DOCTOR WHO KILLED HIS OVERBEARING WIFE FOR THE LOVE OF HIS MISTRESS IS SYNONYMOUS WITH MURDER.

The case of Dr. Crippen was a murder mystery in the classic sense. It had adultery, poison, and an international manhunt. In 1910, England was captivated by the story of this mild-mannered man, his vulgar wife, and his beautiful mistress.

The medical certification and ability of Hawley Harvey Crippen is open to question. An American, he worked in the United States as an eye and ear specialist, but professional standards for doctors didn't exist in the United States at the time. In 1885, he found faintly disreputable employment with a patent medicine company.

Crippen's personal life seems to have been as precarious as his professional one: His second wife was a star-struck woman named Kunigunde Mackamotzki (wisely, she changed her name to Cora) who felt she was destined to become a great singer. To that end, she used the stage name Belle

Elmore. In reality, Cora Crippen was a domineering, ostentatious woman who dwarfed her husband both in size and in personality. Crippen, short in stature with bulging eyes and scrawny mustache, seemed all the more meek when viewed standing next to his hulking Cora.

The couple moved to London in 1900. Crippen's professional qualifications proved inadequate for Britain's stricter laws concerning medical practice at the time. He was obliged to take a job managing the London branch of the patent medicine company that he had moved to London in order to escape. Cora kept at her singing, expanding to music hall performances.

The couple lived at 39 Hilltop Crescent in North London. By 1907, Crippen completely hated his wife and her ideas of middle-class respectability. He was fed up with her self-conscious devotion to opera and with the braggarts who encouraged her. He especially hated that neither his wife nor her friends had the slightest idea of how vulgar they were.

The Crippens' marriage was a sham as well. Cora took a lover, an American entertainer named Bruce Miller. Because Cora imagined that her domination of her husband had stripped him of all will to defy her, Bruce stayed openly at the Crippen household when he visited London.

But Hawley Harvey Crippen had a few surprises

of his own. He had fallen madly in love with his young bookkeeper, Ethel Le Neve, a quiet, lovely, and most demure woman of 24. He began a romantic relationship with Ethel, and as their affair continued, Crippen began to hatch fantastic schemes. Finally, in 1910, he decided to kill his wife.

He obtained five grams of hyoscine, a hypnotic nerve depressant. In early February, he invited several of Cora's theatrical friends over for dinner. As the last of them was leaving, Crippen poisoned his wife and then cleared away the dishes.

Crippen obtained £80 by pawning his wife's jewelry and some of her clothes. The rest of his wife's wardrobe he gave to Ethel. He informed the Music Hall Ladies Guild that Cora had fallen ill and could neither attend nor contribute to their cause. He started stepping out with Ethel, who wore fine clothes that friends knew belonged to Cora.

Rumors and suspicions finally brought the police to Crippen's door with official inquiries. The doctor informed them that his wife had returned to the United States to care for a sick relative, had fallen ill herself, and died in California. The police were satisfied, and the investigation might have been dropped right there. However, Crippen's nerve subsequently broke, and he panicked and ran. When the police discovered that Crippen and

Ethel had left England for Rotterdam, The Netherlands, warrants were issued for their arrest. In addition, Interpol (the International Criminal Police Organization) was informed.

The police also started digging in Crippen's basement at Hilltop Crescent for clues. In the cellar, they found assorted pieces of human flesh. There were parts of a buttock, pieces of skin and muscle, and internal organs. Although the victim's sex could not be conclusively determined, the scar tissue showed that the victim had previously undergone abdominal surgery. These surgical scars matched Cora Crippen's medical history. The international search for Crippen and Le Neve intensified.

Aboard the SS *Montrose*, sailing from Rotterdam to Canada, Captain Kendall noticed that two of his passengers—a Mr. Robinson and his son—were oddly affectionate toward one another. They also looked very much like photos of Crippen and Le Neve that were splashed across the newspapers. Kendall radioed Scotland Yard from the middle of the Atlantic. The authorities were waiting at the dock as the ship pulled into Canadian waters on July 31. Photos of Crippen's dramatic arrest and Ethel Le Neve's peculiar impersonation of a young boy made front-page news worldwide. Upon their arrest, Crippen muttered, "I'm glad it's all over; this business is too nerve-wracking."

With such a sensational arrest, a highly charged trial was assured. The doctor was the first of the two lovers to be put before a jury. His five-day trial opened on October 18, 1910. From the start, it was clear that Crippen had given up all chance of acquittal. Though apparently indifferent to his own fate, he was determined to put forth the innocence of his beloved Ethel, and he swore in open court that she knew nothing of Cora's murder.

Crippen was found guilty and sentenced to death. While awaiting execution, he was much relieved to learn that a jury had acquitted Ethel of any wrongdoing. Dr. Crippen was hanged on November 23, 1910. His last request was that he be buried with a photograph of Ethel.

GORDON F. CUMMINS

THE VICTIM HAD BEEN MUTILATED WITH A RAZOR BLADE OR A CAN OPENER.

For many Londoners in February of 1942, the news stirred memories of Jack the Ripper. Little more than 50 years had passed since the Ripper's reign of terror, and once again, the slashed bodies of women began to appear.

A murderer was stalking the streets at a time when war-weary Londoners spent nights in black-out. Air-raid sirens forced them into shelters, often in the company of total strangers. It was in such a shelter that the fiend made his first kill.

In the early hours of February 9, 1942, Evelyn Margaret Hamilton was found dead in a London air-raid shelter. The 40-year-old teacher had been strangled. The next evening, another woman was found strangled in a Soho apartment building. This second victim, Mrs. Evelyn Oatley, had been mutilated with a razor blade or a can opener.

On February 14, another victim, Mrs. Doris Jouannet, was choked to death with a stocking. Her body had also been slashed with a razor.

Though apparently killed on the same day, the corpse of Mrs. Margaret Florence Lowe wasn't found until three days later, in her apartment. Several scratches were seen on her body. Still, the police lacked the evidence to find the killer.

The next night, February 15, Mrs. Heywood was accosted as she left a pub. She told the police a man tried to force himself on her and kiss her. When she refused, he began to strangle her. She was saved when a passerby intervened and the attacker ran off. This time, however, there was a clue: The strangler left behind a gas mask.

Later that same evening, someone broke into the home of Kathleen King and attempted to strangle her. Neighbors answered her cries for help, and the fiend escaped through a window. Once again he left a clue: the belt of a Royal Air Force cadet. Both the belt and the gas mask bore the same identification number.

Royal Air Force records revealed that the equipment was issued to Gordon Frederick Cummins. Scotland Yard was then able to link Cummins by physical evidence to the crimes. And many of the delays common to criminal proceedings for civilians could be bypassed. Military justice is often swift, especially during a war. In more lenient times, Cummins might have been given psychiatric care. But in time of war that was a luxury. Cummins was hanged on June 25, 1942.

JEFFREY DAHMER

PUTREFIED HANDS TURNED UP IN A COOKING POT, A TRIO OF HEADS IN A FREEZER, FIVE SKULLS IN A BOX AND IN A FILE CABINET.

On Milwaukee's west side is a run-down neighborhood where the police assigned to the area routinely see crime and unpleasantness. But on the evening of July 22, 1991, officers Rolf Mueller and Robert Rauth found more than routine unpleasantness—they found unspeakable horror.

Late in the evening, their patrol car was flagged down by a young black man, handcuffs dangling from his wrist. The young man, whose name was Tracy Edwards, said he had been held captive in an apartment nearby and had been threatened with a butcher knife.

Mueller and Rauth went with Edwards to the Oxford Apartments on North 25th Street. In apartment 213, they were greeted politely by blond-haired, 31-year-old Jeffrey Dahmer.

Officer Mueller searched the bedroom and found the butcher knife Edwards had mentioned.

He also found Polaroid snapshots of men performing homosexual acts and photographs of dead men. Many of the corpses had been dismembered or otherwise mutilated. Then Mueller was horrified to discover that the photos had been taken in the very room in which Mueller stood.

One of the pictures prompted Mueller to stride to the kitchen. At that, Dahmer's calm demeanor suddenly vanished. He became violent and had to be forcibly restrained. Mueller eyed the refrigerator, then opened it. Inside, resting on a lower shelf, was a neatly boxed human head. A killer had been revealed.

Jeffrey Dahmer was catapulted to worldwide infamy. Furthermore, an ugly scandal arose that raised the specters of police incompetence and, worse, institutionalized prejudice.

Later that night, after Dahmer had been led to jail, investigators discovered more body parts. In all, the apartment was littered with the remains of 11 young men. Putrefied hands turned up in a cooking pot, a trio of heads in a freezer, five skulls in a box and in a file cabinet. An industrial-size plastic drum in the bedroom was filled with noxious chemicals and the viscous remains of three bodies. Dahmer had kept a selection of other chemicals, too, including chloroform and formaldehyde. The presence of tools suggested that the corpses had been dismembered with electric saws.

Dahmer quickly confessed to the murders of the 11 men whose remains had been found in his apartment. Later, he confessed to six more killings. Files pertaining to unsolved murders from locations as far away as Germany were reexamined.

Jeffrey Dahmer's confession indicated he had been busy for more than ten years, perfecting his technique and finally turning murder into a grisly assembly-line process. Like a consumer with a carefully prepared list, Dahmer shopped for his victims—most of them black—in Milwaukee and Chicago malls, gay bathhouses, bus stops, and bars. He then lured them to his apartment by offering them money to pose for homosexual pictures. Then he served them drugged drinks, strangled them or slit their throats, and cut apart their bodies. He had had sex with at least one of the corpses.

Even more gruesome revelations followed. Investigators had been puzzled by the absence of food in Dahmer's kitchen—the shelves held nothing but condiments—but things snapped into terrible focus when Dahmer remarked that he had packaged certain body parts "to eat later." He claimed, for instance, to have cut out the bicep of one victim, intending to savor it at his leisure.

The world was horrified by the enormity of Dahmer's crimes; the shock was felt with particular sharpness by Milwaukee's black and gay communities after it became apparent that five of the murders might have been prevented. Incredibly, Milwaukee police had been to Dahmer's apartment in May to follow up on a complaint from black neighbors regarding a naked, bleeding boy running through the streets.

The boy was Konerak Sinthasomphone, a 14-year-old Laotian immigrant whom Dahmer had lured to his apartment and (ineptly) drugged. Police officers confronted Sinthasomphone in the street, listened to his hysterical story, and then returned him to Dahmer's apartment. Although photos of earlier victims littered the place and a human body lay festering in the bedroom, the police failed to notice. They were satisfied that Sinthasomphone was an adult and that the situation was nothing more than what one of the officers called a "boyfriend-boyfriend thing."

Shortly after the officers left Dahmer's apartment, the serial killer strangled his adolescent victim and dismembered the body. Dahmer continued to kill for seven more weeks, notching four additional victims.

Transcripts of police-dispatch recordings made immediately after the May encounter revealed that the investigating officers had made crude sexual jokes about the situation and had almost completely shrugged off the concern shown by the black witnesses. Not unjustifiably, this apparent callous indifference raised the ire of the Milwaukee citizenry. Police chief Philip Arreola found himself at the center of a firestorm of controversy. Besieged by an outraged public and under attack from members of the police force, he later fired two of the officers who returned Sinthasomphone to Dahmer.

The cause of all the upset, Jeffrey Dahmer, remained a puzzlement. Soft-spoken in court, he cooperated with authorities, offering details of his alleged crimes and even drawing investigators a map of the backyard of his boyhood home in Bath, Ohio. There, Dahmer claimed, police would find the shattered bones of his first victim, an 18-year-old hitchhiker named Steven Hicks, whom Dahmer had abducted and murdered in 1978. Sure enough, the site yielded an impressive collection of human bone fragments.

What combination of factors "made" Jeffrey Lionel Dahmer? He grew up in Bath, Ohio, near Akron, the son of comfortably middle-class parents. Like many serial killers, as a boy he was an intelligent underachiever, more apt to clownishly disrupt class than to pay attention to his studies. By the time he was 16, Dahmer was an alcohol abuser who had a perverse interest in chemistry and a penchant for torturing and dismembering animals.

His parents divorced in 1978, when he was a senior in high school. He says he committed his first murder, that of Steven Hicks, in June of that year. His career at Ohio State ended almost as soon as it began, and by 1979 Dahmer was in the Army, stationed in Germany. There, his alcoholism worsened, and he received an early discharge in 1981.

He moved to Milwaukee, where he claims to have killed three men at the home of his grandmother in 1985. Those crimes went undiscovered, but Dahmer did show up on the Milwaukee police blotter for other offenses: urinating in front of children in 1986 and fondling a 13-year-old Laotian boy (ironically, the older brother of Konerak Sinthasomphone) in 1988. The latter transgression earned Dahmer a one-year prison sentence.

Dahmer was paroled after 10 months. He found work in a Milwaukee candy factory and set up housekeeping at the Oxford Apartments, where he resumed—and refined—his hideous avocation. His neighbors, apparently inured to the peculiarities of city life, paid little attention to the awful odors that emanated from apartment 213 or to the late-night whine of Dahmer's power saws.

Two men who had encounters with the killer lived to tell the tale. A 20-year-old Milwaukee man whose name has not been revealed told police of his July 1991 encounter with Jeffrey Dahmer at a laundromat a block and a half from Dahmer's apartment building. "He offered me $75 to spend three hours with him," the man recalled. "He said we would drink some beer, drink some rum. I never went over there."

Like many other men before him, Mississippi native Tracy Edwards, 32, was lured by Dahmer to apartment 213. Beer-drinking led to rougher sport: Dahmer snapped handcuffs around Edwards's wrist and, according to Edwards, tried to kill him with a butcher knife. "It was like confronting Satan himself," Edwards said later. He managed to escape the apartment and run outside, where he stopped a passing patrol car. In an ironic twist, the publicity that surrounded Edwards's adventure alerted Mississippi authorities, who had indicted the former Tupelo resident in November 1990 for sexual battery involving a 14-year-old girl. Edwards was arrested in Milwaukee on August 6, 1991, and held without bail, pending extradition to Mississippi.

The Dahmer story recalls a similar Wisconsin case, that of grave-robber and serial killer Ed Gein. But though Gein lived in isolation on a remote farm, Dahmer resided in proximity to other people and freely divided his time between two large cities. For more than a decade, he walked among innocent men and women, searching for opportunities to throw off his disguise. Of the myriad horrors the Dahmer case invites us to contemplate, this one may be the most unnerving of all.

LAURIE DANN

HER SHOOTING SPREE SHOCKED WINNETKA RESIDENTS AND LEFT SCARS OF UNCERTAINTY.

Winnetka, Illinois, is an affluent Chicago suburb not normally touched by violent crime. On May 20, 1988, Laurie Wasserman Dann, a 30-year-old divorcée, went on a shooting spree that shocked Winnetka residents and left scars of uncertainty.

On that day, Dann walked into a second-grade classroom in the Hubbard Woods Elementary School. The teacher, Amy Moses, gave Dann a seat, thinking she was there to observe the class. But in a few moments, Dann rose without a word and left the room. She entered the boys' lavatory with a gun drawn. First-grader Robert Tross, age six, entered, and Dann shot him in the chest and stomach. She left him on the floor along with the weapon, a .357 Magnum.

Then Dann returned to the classroom, shut the door, and ordered Moses to put all the children in a corner of the room. When the teacher refused, Dann pulled out a small handgun. Moses and Dann struggled; Dann drew another gun. Moses managed to open the door and call for help, but Dann broke free and fired at the children. Four second-graders were seriously wounded. One student, Nicholas Corwin, was killed instantly when he pushed his best friend out of the line of fire.

Dann fled the school and jumped into her car. She accidentally drove a few blocks down a dead-end street and crashed into a tree. After reloading her guns, she ran into a nearby house.

The quick-thinking Dann told the house's residents that she had been assaulted. She said the police were after her for shooting her assailant. One member of the household, 20-year-old Philip Andrew, sensed that something was wrong. He persuaded Dann to make a phone call; she called her parents. After the call, Andrew tried to take Dann's gun, but she shot him in the chest. In the commotion, the other residents hurried outside. Dann then ran upstairs, put the gun in her mouth, and fired. She died instantly. During her rampage, Dann killed one person, besides herself, and wounded six. Later investigations showed that Laurie Dann had a lengthy history of mental illness.

LARRY EYLER

THE POLICE SEARCHED EYLER'S APARTMENT AS WELL AS OTHER ROOMS HE HAD ACCESS TO IN THE APARTMENT COMPLEX. THEY FOUND HUMAN SKIN IN THE LAUNDRY ROOM TUB AND BLOODY WATER IN A BASEMENT BASIN.

On an August day in 1984, the janitor for a large apartment complex in a North Side neighborhood of Chicago watched a muscular man haul several plastic bags from a neighboring building to a nearby trash Dumpster. The janitor took notice of the beefy-looking man because it was obvious by the way he walked that each bundle contained something fairly heavy. After the mysterious man returned to his apartment, the janitor began to feel that something was wrong with this picture. Why hadn't the man used his own building's Dumpster to unload his trash, particularly if the bags were so heavy? What trash items could have possibly weighed so much? Despite his curiosity, the janitor did nothing at that time.

Later, the custodian for the mystery man's apartment complex found the bags in the trash and decided to open them. He made a grim discovery. The plastic bags contained the dismembered body of a teenage boy. The police searched the man's apartment as well as other rooms he had access to in the apartment complex. They found human skin in the tub in the laundry room and bloody water in a basin in the basement.

The brawny man seen carrying the plastic bags was later identified as Larry Eyler, a 31-year-old housepainter. Local authorities had previously figured Eyler as a suspect in the murder of another young man and had even indicted Eyler in that case. In February 1983, a judge had reduced Eyler's one-million-dollar bond to $10,000, an amount that Eyler paid. In August of 1984, he was out of jail on that reduced bond.

The dismembered body in the trash, which had been cut into eight pieces, was what remained of Daniel Bridges. Bridges, who had been sexually abused as a young boy, had spent the last four years of his life as a child prostitute. Somehow Bridges had been lured to Eyler's apartment, where he was murdered. An autopsy revealed that Bridges had died from a stab wound to the back, despite multiple stab wounds to the chest.

Eyler was tried and found guilty of the murder of the Chicago teenager. He was sentenced to death and for years awaited his fate on death row in the Pontiac Correctional Center in north-central Illinois. Investigators then learned that Eyler was also a suspect in 22 other murders of young men and boys in Indiana, Wisconsin, Kentucky, and Illinois.

In October 1990, a Chicago author published the book *Freed to Kill* about Eyler, which led Indiana authorities to reopen the unsolved homicide of a man named Steve Agan. In December, Eyler began to cooperate with the Indiana authorities about the Agan murder in hopes that he would not be executed in Illinois. Eyler told of his involvement in the murder of Steve Agan, a 28-year-old car-wash employee in Terre Haute, Indiana, who was found December 28, 1982, in an abandoned building in a remote area near Newport, Indiana. Agan had been bound, gagged, mutilated, and killed.

After he negotiated a plea bargain with Indiana officials, obtaining a 60-year sentence for his role in Agan's death, Eyler gave a detailed confession. Eyler named Robert David Little, a 52-year-old Indiana State University professor, as his accomplice in killing Agan. The convicted killer gave a specific account of the sexually inspired murder that he and the university professor had committed. After they promised Agan that he would be paid to engage in various homosexual acts, they drove the victim to a barn, where they photographed their step-by-step torture of the helpless Agan. They took turns stabbing the young man until he died.

Eyler had lived with Little in Terre Haute, moving to Chicago in 1983. Between 1982 and 1984, Eyler commuted between Terre Haute and Chicago, and he became accustomed to picking up young men or boys on the highway. He transported them to various rural locations, where he bound, tortured, and killed them usually by multiple stab wounds.

On December 13, 1990, Eyler offered Illinois officials his confession to 20 unsolved murders and agreed to implicate Little in five other killings in exchange for getting his death sentence reduced to life imprisonment. However, Eyler's bid was rejected on January 8, 1991. Eyler remains on death row in the Pontiac Correctional Center in Illinois. In 1991, Little was put on trial for his part in Agan's murder and was acquitted.

RAYMOND MARTINEZ FERNANDEZ AND MARTHA BECK

UNDER A PATCH OF FRESH CONCRETE IN THE CELLAR POLICE FOUND MRS. DOWNING AND HER LITTLE DAUGHTER.

Widowed at the young age of 26, Delphine Downing began to feel the pain and loneliness of a solitary existence about two years after the death of her husband. Hoping to start a new life for herself and find a father for her two-year-old daughter, Rainelle, Downing decided to actively seek a new spouse. She joined a lonely hearts club and began corresponding with potential candidates. Before long, she was writing regularly to a charming 31-year-old man named Charles Martin. His optimistic letters awakened her hopes for a new husband and her dreams for a brighter future. In actuality, she was corresponding with Raymond Martinez Fernandez, and her future was darker than she could ever have imagined.

The relationship began innocently enough.

Fernandez and a woman he introduced as his sister arrived for a visit at Downing's house near Grand Rapids, Michigan, on January 19, 1949. Though not particularly handsome, Fernandez was clean-cut and a snappy dresser. He also exhibited an engaging personality, and he behaved lovingly toward little Rainelle. To the lonely and vulnerable Downing, he seemed to be the key to a happy life.

But all was not as it seemed. He seduced the young woman, though no marriage proposal was forthcoming. Quite rapidly, he began to take over her life. During the following weeks, he became her business agent and arranged for the sale of her properties. His "sister," Martha Beck, an obese and foul-tempered woman, was really the Latin romeo's mistress and accomplice. She became furious at his stalling and renewed pressure on Fernandez to carry out his original plan—to marry and then kill the unsuspecting widow. Ultimately, he didn't bother with the former.

In early March 1949, the mother and her child disappeared from sight. Concerned neighbors called the police. Following through on his suspicions, a deputy by the name of Clarence Randle went to the house when Fernandez and Beck were out. There the police discovered a patch of fresh concrete in the cellar. Randle stated, "We dug until we found Mrs. Downing and her little daughter." When the conspirators returned, they were questioned about the bodies. Fernandez admitted that Mrs. Downing had been given sleeping pills and then shot in the head. The cold-hearted Beck had drowned little Rainelle in a washtub.

Behind bars, Fernandez foolishly bragged that he made his living fleecing lonely women. Further investigation revealed that Mrs. Downing was not his first victim. In fact, the authorities came up with a list of over 20 suspected victims. For example, Jane Thompson had died mysteriously in October 1947 in La Línea, Spain, after a holiday with Fernandez. Back in New York, he first said she had been killed in a train crash. Later Fernandez claimed that she had died from a heart attack. Then he produced a will that gave him claim to Thompson's apartment, which was occupied by her mother. He moved in with her, and then had her evicted, making the apartment exclusively his.

In another scheme, Fernandez married Myrtle Young on August 14, 1948. The newlyweds settled in a boarding house in Chicago, but in no time at all, the couple became a trio. Martha Beck came along as Fernandez's protector, and she immediately took her place in the marital bed. Myrtle objected, so Beck fed her an overdose of barbiturates. Then Beck put Myrtle on a bus to her native Little Rock, Arkansas, where she died in a hospital.

New York was the site of yet another of the

criminal couple's schemes. There the pair took $6,000 from widow Janet Fay. Once again, Fernandez promised marriage. And once again, it was Beck who made the decisive move: "I bashed her head in with a hammer," she admitted to police. Fernandez finished the job by strangling the widow with a scarf. Fernandez and Beck crammed the body into a trunk and buried it in the cellar of a rented house in New York City. Inexplicably, Fernandez confessed over the telephone to the New York district attorney.

After the killing of Delphine Downing and her daughter, Fernandez and Beck were held by the police in Michigan, which did not have the death penalty. New York, which allowed execution for murder, sought to have Fernandez and Beck moved to its jurisdiction to be tried for the slaying of Janet Fay. The deadly duo attempted to evade extradition and remain in Michigan, but failed. New York tried and convicted them, and on March 8, 1951, they were executed at Sing Sing.

ALBERT FISH

STRIPPING HIMSELF NAKED, FISH STRANGLED THE CHILD AND THEN BEHEADED AND DISMEMBERED HER WITH A MEAT CLEAVER. HE THEN COOKED HER BODY PARTS INTO A STEW SEASONED WITH ONIONS AND CARROTS.

Albert Fish had gone gaunt and stringy with age. Sunken-cheeked, with deep-set eyes, he seemed ordinary, harmless. A housepainter and the father of six children, Fish appeared as common as clay. But Albert Fish was a monster—a multiple killer, a child molester, a cannibal. When his horrific career came to an end in 1934, Fish, then 66 years old, was interviewed by a prison psychiatrist who wrote, "There was no known perversion that he did not practice and practice frequently." Fish's confession was so shocking that the prosecuting attorneys—members of a breed usually eager to expose the failings of defendants—could barely bring themselves to read it aloud in court.

Unlike a lot of sexually motivated killers, Fish

did not begin his career while a young man. Instead, he found his avocation when he was 49, after his wife left him in 1917 for another man. Fish underwent a marked change in personality and fell into a pattern of bizarre behavior. He began to clip lonely-hearts advertisements and send obscene replies to the pathetic advertisers. He cultivated an interest in cannibalism and saved news stories about such people as Fritz Haarmann, the "Hanover Vampire."

Fish's masochistic streak came out as well. He claimed to have molested hundreds of children. He enjoyed the experience of physical pain and often pleaded with his own children to beat him. One of his favorite pastimes was to insert sewing needles into his scrotum, savoring the unbelievable agony. Most unspeakable of all, he levied his terrible imagination against children, whom he would lure to his home with promises of sweets and play. He was such a friendly grandfatherly type—what innocent child could resist? Many unfortunate children did not, and thus found themselves the victims of unspeakable tortures practiced by a dedicated sadist.

In 1928, Fish indulged his taste for human flesh on a ten-year-old girl named Grace Budd. She was the daughter of parents who knew and trusted Fish. When Fish offered to take her to a party for children, they let him do so without any misgivings. Instead of a party, however, Fish took Grace to his cottage in Westchester County, New York. Stripping himself naked, Fish strangled the child and then beheaded and dismembered her with a meat cleaver. He then cooked her body parts into a stew seasoned with onions and carrots. Fish consumed this grisly repast down to the last awful morsel.

At first, Grace Budd's parents refused to believe that she was dead. Perhaps, they told themselves, she had simply run away from home. All hopes for her survival were hideously dashed some six years after her disappearance, when they surprisingly received a letter from Albert Fish wherein he explained exactly what he had done to their little girl.

The letter was traced to Fish, and he was apprehended and brought to trial soon thereafter. The jury discounted his insanity plea and sentenced him to death in the electric chair. He was executed at Sing Sing in New York on January 16, 1936. Fish reportedly faced death eagerly. In his final minutes, he remarked that this was "the supreme thrill, the only one I haven't tried." Two massive jolts of electricity were required to finish him off. To this day, he remains the oldest individual to have been put to death in the state of New York.

JOHN WAYNE GACY

IN THE CRAWL SPACE BENEATH THE HOUSE, INVESTIGATORS DISCOVERED SEVERAL BODIES IN SHALLOW GRAVES AND LONG TRENCHES. MANY HAD BEEN COVERED WITH QUICKLIME TO HASTEN THEIR DECAY.

For millions of Americans in the years immediately following World War II, the sparkling new suburbs that grew on the outskirts of every great city held the promise of a new life: a fresh start and a home of one's own. Happiness, the suburbs seemed to say, was within everyone's grasp. Years later, in the 1970s, the suburban lifestyle remained the goal of countless wage-earners. One such suburb is Harwood Heights, Illinois, a quiet, unassuming community of modest homes located northwest of Chicago. An overweight contractor named John Wayne Gacy lived in one of the neat ranch-style homes there. He seemed to embody the American dream, and yet, from 1975 through 1978, Gacy's home was visited by a virtual parade of young men, whom he sexually assaulted, tortured, and brutally murdered.

Much of John Wayne Gacy's life is completely unremarkable. He was born in Chicago on March 17, 1942. He enjoyed a normal childhood, went to business school, and got married. He lived in Iowa for a while. In Waterloo, he managed a fried chicken restaurant. He impressed his neighbors as an upstanding member of the community and a credit to local business. In a world where quiet anonymity is perfectly normal, Gacy seemed more normal than most. But then, at age 26, Gacy was arrested for sexually assaulting a young boy; at last, the mask had begun to slip.

Gacy's trial disclosed that he had forced the handcuffed boy to have sex with him. Gacy had then paid his victim to keep quiet. But the youth testified against him anyway. In response, Gacy hired another young man to beat up the boy.

Gacy's wife divorced him after he was found guilty and sentenced to ten years in an Iowa prison. His good behavior won him an early parole in 1971, and he was placed on probation.

After he moved to Harwood Heights to begin a new life, Gacy remarried and started a construction business, which he ran out of his house. He had been out of prison less than a year when he was arrested for soliciting a juvenile male for sex. But the charges were dropped when his victim failed to appear in court.

Seeking recognition and status, Gacy involved

himself in local politics and various community activities. As in Iowa, he impressed his associates as a generous and caring individual. Gacy frequently donated time and money to help people in need. Occasionally, he dressed up as a clown to entertain children at different social events.

It was all a facade. In fact, Gacy was an ill-tempered sort who quarreled frequently with his second wife and treated his construction company employees badly. In 1975, one employee, John Butkovich, vanished shortly after getting into an argument with Gacy. In 1976, Gacy's wife divorced him and left the house. Not long after that, Gacy employee Greg Godzik disappeared. Gacy himself was frequently seen behind the wheel of his black Oldsmobile, cruising a district of Chicago frequented by homosexual male prostitutes. Many young men from that district made the regrettable decision to go for a ride with Gacy. Most of them survived the encounter, but not without suffering some degree of physical harm. Gacy, they discovered, was a savage brute who liked to inflict pain. Nevertheless, they did not report him to the police.

After Gacy's divorce, neighbors began to see young men enter his Harwood Heights residence at all hours of the day and night. They also noticed that he often worked late at night on the inside of his house, as if he were remodeling it.

In March 1978, 27-year-old Jeffrey Rignall

checked into a Chicago-area hospital in a sadly abused state. Rignall told police that he had been abducted by a fat man in a black Oldsmobile. The man had lured him into the car, then rendered him unconscious with a chloroform-soaked cloth. At the man's house, Rignall claimed to have been sexually assaulted and beaten with a whip. Since Rignall's memory had been fogged by chloroform, he could not pinpoint the location of the house.

Nonetheless, Rignall was determined to find his assailant. He began to stake out the known haunts of the cruising black Oldsmobile. When he finally spotted the vehicle, he copied down the license plate number and gave it to the police. Gacy was arrested and then released after the authorities decided that they lacked sufficient evidence.

Until that time, Gacy had been lucky. But his luck began to change on December 11, 1978. That was the day 15-year-old Robert Piest disappeared. Piest was last seen by his mother when she dropped him off at a pharmacy that Gacy was remodeling. The boy had gone inside the pharmacy to discuss a job offer from Gacy. He never came home. The mother notified the police, and a warrant was obtained to search Gacy's house. The house was permeated with a repugnant odor. Police searchers traced the smell to a crawl space beneath the house, where they found the decomposing bodies of three young men. Gacy was promptly arrested. Once in custody, he confessed to the sexual torture and murder of more than 30 victims.

Investigators returned to Gacy's house and began to remove the floors. In the crawl spaces beneath the house, they discovered several bodies in shallow graves and long trenches. Many of the bodies had been covered with quicklime to hasten their decay. The house was razed, and more bodies were found. A total of 28 corpses were eventually unearthed. Gacy admitted to having dumped five additional bodies in the nearby Des Plaines River. He had used the river, he explained, when the crawl spaces became filled to capacity. In all, Gacy had murdered 33 victims.

Medical examiners later noted that many of the victims apparently had been strangled, while some had underwear stuffed in their mouths. The amount of physical evidence against Gacy was overwhelming. He went to trial in March 1980 and pleaded not guilty by reason of insanity. Nobody bought Gacy's insanity plea, and he was found guilty and sentenced to die in the electric chair.

The means of execution for condemned criminals in Illinois has changed since 1980. Lethal injection has replaced the electric chair. Until the execution of James Walker in September 1990, no execution had occurred in Illinois since 1962. John Wayne Gacy still awaits his fate on death row.

GERALD GALLEGO

PUBLIC OUTRAGE AGAINST GALLEGO'S DEVIATE SEX CRIMES WAS SO GREAT THAT PEOPLE SENT IN MONEY TO HELP PAY FOR HIS TRIAL.

The perverted crimes of Gerald Gallego, Jr., were discovered after he murdered a 22-year-old college couple, Craig Miller and Mary Beth Sowers, in Sacramento, California, in 1980. He shot Miller soon after abducting the couple, but brought Sowers back to his apartment and raped her before taking her life. Gallego's wife, Charlene, assisted.

Friends of the victims saw them enter the Gallegos' car on the night of the murders, and this information led police to seek out the Gallegos in connection with the crimes. The couple fled, but they were captured in Omaha on November 17.

The couple's morbid history was finally revealed when Charlene, Gallego's sixth wife, eventually agreed to testify against her husband. She was with him in 1978 when he reportedly began a string of sex crimes—all beginning with rape and sexual domination and ending in murder for as many as eight other young women. Charlene described in detail various abductions, rapes, and murders of women ranging in age from 13 to 34.

In April 1983, Gallego was found guilty of murdering Miller and Sowers and sentenced to death in California. But he went on to face murder charges in neighboring Nevada for kidnapping two 17-year-old girls, Karen Chipman and Stacy Redican, from a mall in Reno and driving them to Pershing County, where he sexually abused them and then beat them to death with a blunt instrument.

The Nevada authorities received almost unprecedented cooperation from California officials in putting together the case against Gallego. California has a liberal reputation in death penalty cases; in the early 1980s the California Supreme Court ordered retrials in 18 of the 20 cases of those who appealed death sentences. Even California law enforcement officials publicly admitted their concern in the Gallego case. Nevada did not have the same liberal high court. That state had executed a prisoner less than five years previously, and its high court had been upholding recent death sentences.

There was some concern, however, over the cost of the Nevada trial. It was to take place in the small town of Lovelock, where the girls' bodies had been left by Gallego, and the high legal costs were greater than the local courts could handle. The public became involved when a Sacramento columnist, Stan Gilliam, suggested that people should contribute to the cost of the trial. Contribute they did. Notes and checks started pouring in, most in $5 and $10 increments. All told, more than $20,000 was collected. Some contributors, from as far away as Ohio, enclosed notes. "When you find Gallego guilty . . . pour gasoline on him and burn him alive." Or "If you need a volunteer to push the switch for his execution, let me know."

Gallego was found guilty in the kidnapping and murders of Chipman and Redican and was sentenced to death. Today he waits on Nevada's death row for his execution. His wife was sentenced to 16 1/2 years in prison.

ROBIN GECHT

THE SATANIC CULT REQUIRED WOMEN TO SEVER ONE
OF THEIR OWN BREASTS. THE FOUR MEN EACH ATE
A BITE BEFORE STORING THE BREAST IN A TROPHY
BOX.

In 1982, police were searching for a Jack-the-Ripper
killer who was attacking prostitutes and other
young women in suburban Chicago. The horrors
that were eventually uncovered surpassed their
worst expectations.

The first to vanish was 28-year-old Elmhurst resident Linda Sutton on May 23, 1981. When police
found her body, minus her left breast, in a field
near the Rip Van Winkle Motel in Villa Park, they
figured she was kidnapped by a sadist, but had little by way of clues. The second victim, 21-year-old
Lorraine Borowski, disappeared nearly one year
later, on May 15, 1982. The contents of her purse
were found strewn outside the door of her office in
Elmhurst, but her body was not found until five
months later, in a cemetery near Villa Park. Only
two weeks passed before another victim disap-

peared. Shui Mak, missing from Hanover Park on May 29, was found four months later in Barrington.

But the police investigation into the mutilation deaths of the three suburban women was going nowhere until June 13, 1982, when a 19-year-old prostitute from St. Louis was picked up by Robin Gecht, a 28-year-old self-employed electrician. When police found Angel York, she had been dumped on the side of the road and had one breast slashed open, but she was alive.

She later said she was happy when Gecht picked her up because the police were out in force arresting hookers. However, that glee soon turned to horror when Gecht forced her at gunpoint into the back of his van, handcuffed and bound her, and sexually assaulted her. She testified that Gecht then placed a knife in her hand and ordered her to stab herself in the left breast. He used a bucket to catch the blood as he enlarged the wound, first with his hand and then with a butcher knife. And before dumping her off, he again sexually assaulted her.

But even with one surviving victim, police had not closed their case. Two more women would disappear, including Carole Pappas, the 42-year-old wife of a Chicago Cubs pitcher, before the big break came.

On October 6, the nude body of 20-year-old prostitute Beverly Washington was found beside a

Chicago railroad track. Washington's left breast had been amputated and her right one deeply slashed, but like York, she was alive. From her hospital bed, unable to talk because of tubes in her nose and mouth, Washington scribbled a note describing the red van Gecht drove. He had picked her up in the same neighborhood where York was grabbed. Washington said she was drugged and raped and was unconscious when the mutilation occurred.

Police spotted the van, then driven by 21-year-old Edward Spreitzer, Gecht's friend and helper in his electrician business, on October 20. Gecht was arrested the same day.

Police charged Gecht with the attack on Washington, but they were unable to positively connect him to the murders and he was released on bail. But the police identified Thomas Kokoraleis, his brother Andrew, Spreitzer, and Gecht as renting adjoining rooms at the Rip Van Winkle Motel several months before the Sutton murder. The Kokoraleis brothers had actually left a forwarding address.

Shortly after police picked Tom up for questioning, he cracked. The four men had taken captive women to a bedroom at Gecht's residence, where the group had a "Satanic chapel." The cultic rituals involved forcing the women to sever their own breasts and then gang-raping and killing them. The men celebrated the sacrifice by eating chunks of the breasts before retiring them to a trophy box, which Kokoraleis said at one point held 15 breasts. Police searched Gecht's residence and found the Satanic chapel described by Kokoraleis.

All four were arrested on November 5, 1982. Each was charged with multiple offenses, ranging from kidnapping to rape to murder to deviant sexual assault.

Spreitzer was convicted of four murders and other related crimes in April 1984 and received four life sentences. He later was convicted of the Sutton killing and given the death penalty. Tom Kokoraleis was convicted of the Borowski murder in May 1984 and sentenced to life in prison. Andrew Kokoraleis was convicted of killing Rose Davis, who was found stabbed and strangled with her left breast amputated on September 8, 1982. He received a life sentence on March 18, 1985.

On March 2, 1983, Gecht was convicted of multiple counts of attempted murder, rape, and aggravated battery and sentenced to 120 years in prison in September 1983.

ED GEIN

IN A SHED ATTACHED TO THE MAIN HOUSE, GEIN
DREW AND QUARTERED HIS PRIZED TROPHIES AS IF
THEY WERE SLAUGHTERHOUSE CATTLE. PORTIONS OF
THE QUARTERED CORPSES OFTEN WOUND UP ON HIS
DINNER TABLE.

Wisconsin is hunters' country, heavily wooded,
with many farms and homes isolated and removed
from the sight of neighbors.

Hunting season always causes a stir in upper
Wisconsin. Blood is in the air, and that's usually
the way the locals like it. At least, that was how
they liked it in the Wisconsin town of Plainfield
until 1957, when a local farmer named Ed Gein
was revealed as one of the most bizarre killers in
American history.

Gein (rhymes with lean) was born in Wisconsin
in 1906 and lived the hardy life of a farmer's son.
When his alcoholic father died in 1940, Gein and
his brother Henry took over the farm, living there
with their mother. By all accounts, Mrs. Gein was a

domineering woman who kept a tight emotional rein on both of her sons. She preferred that her boys remain unmarried, and they did. To her, women were evil things that trafficked in the sins of the flesh. She instilled this belief in Ed and Henry, making sure that their energies were confined to seed-planting of the agricultural sort.

As was the case with many small farms in the area, the Gein place did not prosper. A fire broke out one day and Henry fought it so hard that he collapsed and died. Mrs. Gein was felled by a terrible stroke in 1944 and died of a second, even more serious attack in December of 1945.

Then 39 and left alone, Ed withdrew from reality. His mind developed strange fantasies. He became a voracious reader of anatomical texts, and he developed a new interest in women. Then, without explanation, he sealed off all of the farmhouse except for his bedroom and the kitchen.

Because he qualified for a government subsidy, Gein was able to suspend all farm work. To earn extra money he did odd jobs (including baby-sitting) for Plainfield townsfolk and helped out other farmers.

Alone and independent, Ed Gein began to pursue a new vocation: grave robbing. He began exhuming the bodies of women buried in the remote areas of graveyards. Covered by the darkness, Gein dug up the corpses and dragged them to his farm. There, in a shed attached to the main house, Gein drew and quartered his prized trophies as if they were slaughterhouse cattle. Portions of the quartered corpses often wound up on his dinner table.

Gein carried on his macabre adventures until he tired of amusing himself with bodies of long-dead women. He turned to livelier game.

In early November 1957, Gein repeatedly visited the Worden hardware store in Plainfield. Bernice Worden's son, Frank, co-owned the store with his mother. Gein frequently talked with Frank about hunting. The deer season was starting and Gein was very curious about Frank's hunting plans. When Frank said that he would go hunting on Saturday morning, November 16, Gein told Frank that he'd stop by the store that same day to buy some antifreeze.

When Frank returned to the store late Saturday, he was surprised to find the front door locked. Inside, he discovered a pool of blood on the floor. Alarmed by his mother's unexplained absence, he looked closer and found a sales slip in her handwriting made out to Gein for some antifreeze. Worden remembered Gein's earlier remark and called the sheriff to report his mother missing. Frank suggested that Gein be contacted immediately.

Gein was found at the home of Bob and Irene

Hill, a friendly couple who often invited the quiet farmer to dinner. The group had finished eating and Ed was in his car by the time Officer Dan Chase and Deputy "Poke" Spees arrived. Chase asked Gein several questions; Gein's answers indicated that he knew Bernice Worden was dead. The lawman truly believed that Gein was involved, so he arrested Gein.

Meanwhile, Captain Lloyd Schoephoerster of nearby Green Lake County, along with Sheriff Arthur Schley, drove to Gein's farm. Inside the woodshed, they found Bernice Worden. Her body had been butchered like a deer and hung upside down, suspended from the shed's rafters by ropes attached to wooden dowels that had been driven through the backs of her heels. The body had been vertically split from clavicle to pubis, the internal organs removed, and the empty cavity sprayed out with water. Bernice's severed head, found nearby, showed that she had been killed by a gunshot.

An expanded search uncovered the remains of Mary Hogan, a saloon keeper who had disappeared nearly three years before. The lawmen also found that Gein had used various parts from his female victims to "decorate" his house. Human lips had been used to fashion a pull-cord for a windowshade. A shoebox filled with cured and salted human vulvas was discovered; some of the organs had been spray-painted. Mummified heads, some of them adorned with lipstick and other cosmetics, lined one wall. Body parts had been wrapped and stored in Gein's refrigerator, and a nasty-looking human stew simmered on the stove. Human skulls topped Gein's bedposts; others had been sliced and turned into bowls. Most absurdly, a cup of noses sat on the kitchen table. But the greatest horror was upstairs in Gein's closet, where he kept the dried skin of his late mother. It was later revealed that Gein often dressed in his mother's clothes and strapped her body parts over them. Sometimes, thus attired, he would run outside to dance in the moonlight. As the grisly evidence was uncovered at Gein's home during that first awful day of discovery, investigators determined that 15 women had ended up as souvenirs in Gein's house of horrors.

Near Christmas 1957, the court found Gein criminally insane and ordered him sent to Wisconsin's Central State Hospital for the Insane. Based on an expert conclusion ten years later that Gein could stand trial and defend himself, a petition was made for his release from the hospital. In January 1968, a judge ruled that Gein suffered from mental disease and that he should be returned to the Central State Hospital. Gein spent the remainder of his days there. He died of natural causes in 1984.

For Plainfield, Wisconsin, the horror of Ed Gein's crimes was something to be blocked out and forgotten. Indeed, so great was the community's antipathy that the Gein farm burned to the ground under mysterious circumstances not long after Gein's crimes were discovered. But to other observers, Gein became a source of fascination.

"Sick jokes" based on Gein's proclivities became common in schoolyards in Wisconsin and, later, across the nation. The Ed Gein "death car" was snatched up by promoters, and it toured fairs and carnivals for some years after the crimes. In Milwaukee, a writer named Robert Bloch followed the Gein case and was inspired to use it as a springboard for a novel entitled *Psycho*. The book, of course, became the basis for the famous 1960 movie thriller directed by Alfred Hitchcock. Like Gein, Bloch's central character, Norman Bates, was a tortured, murderous neurotic who had been unhealthily dominated by his mother. His mental illness was expressed via murder and an unorthodox sort of taxidermy.

It can be argued that the Gein story inspired the whole crazy quilt of horror films of the late 1970s and early 1980s that dealt with rural nut cases who committed murder with a sick twist. Few will deny that Ed Gein has found a place in the dark side of the national consciousness.

GARY GILMORE

THE CONVICTED KILLER GOT HIS WISH—HE WAS THE FIRST PERSON TO BE EXECUTED IN THE UNITED STATES IN MORE THAN TEN YEARS.

Born in Texas on December 4, 1940, Gary Gilmore was raised in Portland, Oregon. He was always in trouble as a child. He hated his alcoholic father, but was very fond of his mother and younger brother. Their love, however, was not enough to keep the young Gary out of trouble.

At 12, he stole cars and robbed homes along his paper route. At 14, he was stealing guns and trying unsuccessfully to join an adult criminal gang. He was soon convicted of auto theft and sent to reformatory school for 18 months. There he learned even more criminal tricks.

Following his release from the reformatory, Gilmore continued to get into trouble. Intelligent and artistically gifted (he had a genuine flair for painting and drawing), he nevertheless seemed incapable of turning his life around. By age 22, a robbery conviction had netted him a 15-year term in a federal prison, where psychiatrists labeled him a "classic sociopath" who presented a significant threat to society.

Gilmore was paroled in April 1976. He moved to Orem, Utah, where relatives provided him with a job and a place to live. He was soon drinking heavily and devouring pain killers. But neither alcohol nor drugs could calm his raging spirit. On the night of July 19, 1976, he drove to a local gas station armed with a .22 caliber pistol. There he confronted the attendant, a 24-year-old law student named Max Jensen, with a demand for money. Jensen gave him $150. Gilmore then ordered Jensen into the toilet, instructed him to kneel, and fired two bullets into his brain, killing him.

The next day Gilmore drove to Provo in search of his estranged girlfriend, Nicole Baker. Needing more money, he parked his car at a gas station and walked two blocks to a motel. The motel clerk on duty was Bennie Bushnell, age 25. After robbing Bushnell at gunpoint, Gilmore forced the frightened young man to lie facedown on the floor and shot him in the back of the head.

Once outside, Gilmore accidentally shot himself in the hand as he threw his gun into a bush. When he returned to the gas station to pick up his car, the attendant saw Gilmore's bloody hand and notified the police. Gilmore was arrested a short time later. Tried and convicted on two counts of murder, he soon found himself back in prison, this time on Utah's death row.

Against his lawyers' advice, Gilmore appeared before the Utah Supreme Court, which was to hear his appeal. Instead of fighting for his life, however, Gilmore arrogantly informed the justices that he had been given a fair trial. Moreover, he insisted that his sentence be carried out as soon as possible. Four out of five judges ruled in his favor. Gilmore was then given a choice: execution by hanging or by firing squad. Gilmore chose the bullet over the rope. Yet he tried to hasten the hour of his death by twice overdosing on drugs after making a suicide pact with his girlfriend, Nicole.

Gilmore's impending execution became the focus of a media circus in which Gilmore himself was the star attraction. He relished the attention. Gilmore ensured his lasting fame by selling the rights to his story to journalist Lawrence Schiller. Author Norman Mailer also got involved, and his subsequent Pulitzer Prize-winning book about Gilmore, *The Executioner's Song*, was eventually made into a movie.

By that time Gilmore was dead. His execution occurred on January 17, 1977. He was strapped to a chair in the compound of the Utah state prison and shot by four Salt Lake City policemen armed with rifles. It was the first execution in the United States in more than ten years.

DELFINA AND MARIA DE JESUS GONZALES

THE GIRLS THEY COERCED INTO PROSTITUTION EITHER DIED FROM EXTREME ABUSE OR WERE KILLED WHEN THEY LOST THEIR BEAUTY.

In 1963, police in western Mexico investigated reports of girls who disappeared after they accepted jobs as maids. One 16-year-old, Maria Hernandez, dropped from sight after catching a bus to take such a job. The description of the woman who offered the job to Maria led to the arrest of Josefina Gutierrez. Gutierrez admitted to enticing young girls for brothel owners Delfina and Maria de Jesus Gonzales. Gutierrez received up to $70 for each girl.

Investigators traced the Gonzales sisters to a ranch northwest of Mexico City near the city of León in the state of Guanajuato. In December 1963, Mexican police raided the ranch, which was way off the beaten path and could be reached only over a rocky trail. It was surrounded by a high fence, and the entrance was manned by an armed guard. The ranch was a flourishing brothel where captive teenage girls were forced into prostitution. Thirteen girls were being held prisoner in various rooms. The girls looked as though they had once been pretty, but they were now ravaged by sexual and drug abuse, torture, and forced prostitution.

A horror story was literally unearthed on the Rancho El Angel. The police found the buried remains of 80 girls, 11 men, and many newborn babies. The girls either died from extreme abuse or were killed when they lost their beauty. The male murder victims were migratory workers who had returned to Mexico from the United States. When the workers visited the brothel, they were given doped drinks and then slain for their season's wages. The babies had been unwanted infants born to the girls.

The Gonzales sisters heard about the raid and went into hiding. They planned to flee to the United States, but they were arrested before they could leave Mexico. Both women were convicted and received 40-year prison sentences. Other accomplices, including police involved in the corruption, also received long sentences. The Gonzales's fortune was given to victims and their relatives as compensation.

THE GREEN RIVER KILLER

THE GREEN RIVER KILLER STILL HAS NO NAME. POLICE SUSPECT THE SAME PERSON COMMITTED MORE THAN 40 MURDERS, BUT NO ARREST WAS EVER MADE.

Many desperate young women went to the Sea-Tac Highway, an area near the Seattle-Tacoma Airport, looking to make some money. It was a seamy side of town, the road lined with cheap hotels frequented by prostitutes and their tricks. It was also the last place several of the victims of the man still known only as the Green River Killer were seen alive.

The Green River, as it flows in Washington state southward, is not a grand waterway. Brown and murky in some spots, the river and its banks were used sometimes as a dumping ground for the killer. The first victim was 16-year-old Wendy Coffield, found in July 1982. Coffield's body was discovered under a bridge by two boys on a bicycle ride. Within the next few weeks, police had found four more bodies.

Police believe the killings were all done by one man, a man who spent the next two years on a murder spree, killing as many as 48 women. Some of the bodies were not discovered until many years later. The body of Debra Estes was not discovered until late spring of 1988. A teenage runaway, she had been missing since 1982. The killer's victims had several things in common. All were women. All were young. And most were involved in some sort of prostitution.

To police, the series of murders was a case study in frustration. A task force consisting of representatives of the Seattle Police Department, the King County Sheriff's Department, the FBI, Washington State Police and several other local departments was formed. In 1984, the task force spent $200,000 on a mini-computer and a specially designed computer program to sort through and make sense of the more than a million pieces of information gathered by investigators. The task took nearly two years, but police still did not have their killer.

In fact, it was not until 1989 that police announced it had a "viable suspect" in custody, a 38-year-old former law student named William Jay Stevens II. After a television program titled *Manhunt* had featured the Green River Murders, police received a tip that Stevens, in his last year as a student at Gonzaga University Law School in Spokane, was the murderer. Stevens had disappeared from a 1981 work-release program where he was serving a sentence on a 1979 conviction for stealing police equipment.

Police had long held the theory that the Green River Killer made his victims believe he was a police officer. Most damaging to Stevens was that upon a search of his parents' home, they found a police car, dozens of police badges, nearly 30 guns, and more than two dozen license plates.

Although Stevens professed his innocence, police also discovered through credit-card receipts that Stevens had been near 17 of the murder sites. In addition, Stevens was known to tell acquaintances he was working with Seattle police torturing prostitutes.

However, Stevens's family also produced credit-card receipts proving Stevens was vacationing on the East Coast during the summer of 1982, when the first victims were found. As a result, police released him but stated that Stevens was still "a person of interest."

Although no known Green River killings have occurred since 1984, police have not given up on finding the killer. The size of the task force has been cut by 75 percent, most citizens of the Seattle-Tacoma area have lost interest in the case, and prostitutes have long since gone back to working the Sea-Tac Highway. But police say that the Green River Killer will be found.

BELLE GUNNESS

SHE MAY HAVE COLLECTED $30,000 FROM HER BEAUS, WHO NEVER LEFT HER FARM ALIVE.

Belle Gunness's second husband, Peter, was a butcher. He died in 1904, when a falling meat grinder struck him in the head. Belle was now a widow with three children and a hog farm near LaPorte, Indiana. One of the Gunness children blurted out in school, "My momma killed my poppa," which caused a little gossip, but nothing came of it.

After a suitable period of mourning, Belle took her handyman, Ray Lamphere, as her lover. A weak man and an alcoholic, Ray was completely under Belle's thumb. But Belle was also actively looking for new boyfriends. She placed advertisements in the lonely-hearts columns. New gentlemen friends would appear at the farm, and Belle would parade them around in LaPorte. None of these new beaus seemed to stay long. As suddenly as they appeared, they would disappear.

In 1908, Belle received a reply to her lonely-hearts ads from Andrew Helgelien of South

Dakota. Taken with her romantic literary style and her pleas to meet him, he set up a meeting. As an afterthought, she asked if he could bring $1,000 to help her pay her mortgage. The townsfolk promptly noticed Belle's new beau, but he soon vanished like all the rest. Then Belle went to Sheriff Smutzer to complain that her handyman threatened to burn down the farm if she didn't quit seeing her suitors. She had fired Ray Lamphere, but he was in love and he kept hanging around.

Shortly thereafter, on April 28, 1908, a fire totally destroyed Belle's farmhouse. Four bodies were found: Belle's three children and the decapitated body of a woman believed to be Belle. The coroner assumed that the poor woman's head had been cut off by a wooden support that had fallen. Amazingly, he decided to overlook the fact that the corpse weighed 150 pounds, while Belle was a solid woman of 280. The sheriff arrested Ray Lamphere on the charges of arson and murder. When Ray snapped out of a drunken stupor, he loudly professed his innocence. Meanwhile, Asle Helgelien popped up to inquire what had become of his brother Andrew.

The coroner had ordered the workmen to keep digging for the missing head. Though they never found it, 14 other corpses, including the missing Helgelien brother, turned up. The bodies had been cut up by someone who knew how to butcher.

Then the pieces were packaged and hidden in the ground under the house. A police investigation later revealed that Belle might have taken as much as $30,000 from these men, collectively. A more intense search of the ruins turned up several gold rings and Belle's plate for her false teeth. That seemed to satisfy most people that the headless corpse was indeed Belle. They didn't care that the body was "missing" 130 pounds.

Ray Lamphere was convicted of arson. Still claiming that he was innocent, he died in jail. He maintained that Belle had killed a prostitute from nearby Chicago by giving her poison and beheading her. According to Ray, Belle then ripped out her own dental plate for evidence and fled to Chicago with her booty. Some LaPorte residents did claim to have seen her in Chicago on their outings to that city. However, no definite proof of this was ever found.

JOHN GEORGE HAIGH

HE MADE AN INCISION INTO AN ARTERY WITH A PENKNIFE, FILLED A GLASS WITH THE FRESH BLOOD, AND DRANK IT.

The Onslow Court Hotel, in a fashionable part of London, was patronized by well-to-do retired people with money in the bank. In 1949, a small-time thief and con man named John George Haigh, age 39, moved into this hotel posing as an engineer who owned his own factory.

His new neighbors found him affable and friendly, but he became especially friendly with Mrs. Olivia Durand-Deacon, a 69-year-old widow whose husband had left her £40,000. In fact, Haigh told Mrs. Durand-Deacon that his factory could make prototypes of a new product she had designed—plastic fingernails.

On February 18, 1949, Haigh and Mrs. Durand-Deacon traveled 30 miles to an industrial building, part of which he rented for "experiments." Once they were alone, Haigh killed the woman with a shot in the neck from a .38 revolver. According to his own account, he then made an incision into an artery with a penknife, filled a glass with the fresh blood, and drank it.

Haigh stripped the body and stuffed it into a 40-gallon drum designed to hold corrosive material. He then filled the drum with sulfuric acid. Experience had shown him just the right amount to use. The remains of Mrs. Durand-Deacon began to dissolve.

Haigh's scheme was to transfer Mrs. Durand-Deacon's assets to himself over a period of time through careful forgeries. In order for this plan to work, however, it was essential that her disappearance not be noticed quickly. If a relative or friend were to inquire later on, he could claim she was traveling on vacation. This was the method he had employed with five other victims over the past several years.

This time, however, a neighbor at the hotel noticed Mrs. Durand-Deacon's absence the day after the murder. Furthermore, this woman—Mrs. Constance Lane—had been told by Mrs. Durand-Deacon of her plan to visit Mr. Haigh's factory. Haigh claimed that she never showed up for the appointment and pretended to be concerned. By the next day, Mrs. Lane's apprehension was such that Haigh felt obliged to accompany her to the police and file a missing person's report.

At first, the police had no reason to doubt

George Haigh's account. They began a simple, routine investigation. A check into Haigh's background alerted police that he had already served three prison terms for fraud and robbery. Within a few days, the police had found Haigh's "laboratory." The only evidence noticed there was a recently fired revolver and blood on the floor. Without a body, no case could be made. At that point, the police were not well-enough informed to rake through the pile of acidic sludge that had recently been dumped out. They were, however, ready to question Mr. Haigh a little more intensely.

"Requested" to give further evidence, Haigh soon concluded that the jig was up. He began to volunteer evidence, and was quite a bit more helpful than the police expected. When he told them the part about drinking the victim's blood, the police began to sense that Haigh was laying the groundwork for an insanity defense. They analyzed the sulfuric sludge and found bone fragments and enough of Mrs. Durand-Deacon's bridgework to make a positive identification. The authorities then charged Haigh with murder.

Aware that Haigh would claim insanity, the prosecution kept a low profile on the case and made sure that every legal step was properly taken. With all these precautions, they were understandably horrified when the March 4, 1949, London *Daily Mirror* trumpeted: "VAMPIRE—A

MAN HELD." Haigh had leaked his story to the press. The editor of the *Daily Mirror* was fined £10,000 and given three months in jail as punishment for pretrial publicity and as a warning to other newspapers. The trial proceeded uneventfully. Though the defense claimed insanity and played up Haigh's blood-drinking, the jury was unmoved. It took them only 15 minutes to return a guilty verdict with the death penalty mandated.

REVEREND EDWARD WHEELER HALL AND ELEANOR MILLS

THE CREATIVE MURDER OF ILLICIT LOVERS LED TO MUCH SPECULATION AND SENSATIONAL NEWS COVERAGE.

In a picturesque apple orchard off a New Brunswick, New Jersey, back road on September 17, 1922, two bodies were found. It was an unusual sight, since both of the victims were neatly dressed and composed. The man, clothed in a dark blue suit and clerical collar, had a Panama hat placed over his head as if to shield him from the sun. In his arms lay a well-dressed woman in a bright blue and red polka-dot dress. Her legs were crossed and her dress was pulled down as far as the material would allow. Even her face was modestly covered with a scarf. The setting was oddly unsettling, especially since beneath the hat and scarf were bullet holes from a .32-caliber gun.

Further inspection showed that the man had been shot once through the brain. In contrast, the woman had been shot three times in the face, and her throat was slashed. Strewn around the bodies were passionate love letters that had apparently been exchanged by the now-dead lovers. Most interesting of all, however, was the personal calling card that was propped up against the dead man's feet. He was identified as Reverend Edward Wheeler Hall, pastor of a very wealthy and well-respected Episcopalian church in town. As serene as the lovers appeared at first glance, there was no doubt that the killer was trying to leave an entirely different message. The person(s) responsible for this double murder wanted everyone to know the identity of the pair, as well as their relationship. Mrs. Eleanor Mills, the wife of the church's janitor and a member of the congregation's choir, was later identified as the woman. The killer did not offer to name her as had been done with the Reverend Hall. Apparently, they were lovers for several years—Reverend Hall was 41; Mrs. Mills was 34. It was truly amazing that no one suspected the two of having an affair, particularly when the man was a prominent minister in a small town.

In contrast with the after-the-fact delicacy of the murder scene, it appeared that a great deal of passion and vengeance had been vented by the killer: Closer examination of Mrs. Mills's throat revealed that the former singer's tongue, larynx, and windpipe had been cut out.

The New Brunswick police were ill prepared to investigate such a crime. No autopsies were ever performed. No detailed search of the crime scene was ever made. The police forgot to cordon off the scene from the public, so within days the orchard was so overrun with curious onlookers and souvenir hunters that any investigation was impossible. In the absence of an official investigation, reporters from New York City—engaged at that time in an anything-goes circulation war—were only too happy to fill the void.

Reporters swarmed New Brunswick. They interviewed Mr. Mills, a small, retiring man who seemed confused by the whole, horrible situation. The reporters questioned the Mills's teenage daughter, a jazz-baby flapper who craved notoriety and proved herself to be willing to say anything.

Mrs. Hall, the reverend's widow, made herself unavailable for comment. However, her half-witted brother, Willie Stevens—who collected bugs and hung around the fire department—was good for tantalizing copy. Mrs. Hall was a wealthy socialite, a plain, plump-faced woman eight years her husband's senior. Her standing in the New Brunswick community was unquestioned. When she let it be known among her friends that she wanted the circus to be over, a grand jury (composed mainly of prominent New Brunswickers and close friends of Mrs. Hall) was quickly convened.

The grand jury heard what little evidence there was, but refused to even call Mrs. Hall to testify. The grand jury then closed the case, pronouncing it unsolved. The police were happy to let the matter drop, and the reporters had no avenues left to pursue. Mrs. Hall herself promptly sailed to Europe for an extended vacation. However unsatisfactorily, the matter seemed to have been settled.

Four years later, in the midst of another New York circulation war that sent newspaper reporters in search of sensational material, the *New York Mirror* decided to stir the ashes of the Hall-Mills case. Much evidence had been lost to souvenir hunters, but the papers knew that a persistent investigator with an expense account might pry something loose. And that's exactly what happened. The *Mirror* came into possession of the calling card that had been left at the feet of Reverend Hall's corpse, and had it tested for fingerprints. The prints on the card were those of Mrs. Hall's half-witted brother, Willie Stevens. Because of this evidence (and a threat of adverse publicity), the governor of New Jersey reopened the case. Four people were arrested and charged with murder: Mrs. Hall; Willie Stevens; another brother, Henry Stevens (an aristocratic gentleman who was an expert shot); and a cousin, Wall Street financier Henry Carpender.

The trial was dubbed "The Trial of the Century,"

and was emphatically covered by every newspaper in the country. Nearly 100 reporters, including Damon Runyon, jammed the little courthouse daily. It was estimated that over 12 million words per day were filed with the country's newspapers during the trial's 22-day run.

The case of the prosecution hinged on three points: The love letters, which established a deep and lasting love between the two victims; the fingerprint evidence, which placed Willie Stevens at the scene of the crime; and the testimony of Mrs. Jane Gibson, an eyewitness who lived next to the orchard. Mrs. Gibson was dubbed "the Pig Woman" because she raised hogs and due to her backward, countrified ways. She claimed to have heard arguing voices and gunshots on the day of the murders, and to have seen Mrs. Hall's Dodge sedan parked nearby. This impressive testimony was made all the more compelling because the Pig Woman—dying of cancer—literally delivered her remarks from a deathbed that was hauled into the courtroom. Nevertheless, members of the local jury regarded Mrs. Gibson as something of a buffoon, and they resented the intrusion of the newspapermen and the seeming arrogance of the upstate state's attorney who prosecuted the case. The jury deliberated for six hours and brought back verdicts of not guilty for all four defendants. So it is that the murder of Reverend Hall and the younger woman who loved him remains—at least officially—unsolved.

After her acquittal, the vindicated Mrs. Hall filed a three-million-dollar libel suit against the *New York Mirror*, which had been convicting her twice daily on their front pages for six months. Embarrassingly, during the trial, the managing editor of the *New York Mirror* had dared Mrs. Hall in print to sue his paper. When she took him up on his challenge, the *Mirror* was forced to settle out of court, reputedly for a large amount.

JEAN HARRIS

CAN A GUN GO OFF ACCIDENTLY THREE TIMES? DR. TARNOWER'S DESPONDENT LOVER CLAIMED THAT IT DID ON THE NIGHT OF HIS DEATH.

At 56, Jean Harris was a very unhappy woman on the night of March 10, 1980. It seemed that every part of her life was causing her grief. Her job was in trouble. After expelling three students for smoking marijuana at the Madeira School where she was headmistress, she was called before the board of supervisors. She believed that her lover of 14 years, Dr. Herman Tarnower, was leaving her for a younger woman. And Jean Harris certainly did not want to lose the prominent physician and author of *The Scarsdale Medical Diet*.

Jean Harris was so despondent that she was suicidal. She wrote a new will, wrote a suicide note, and packed a loaded gun with five shells into her purse. All she wanted to do was to say goodbye to Tarnower before she took her own life in the garden of his home.

According to Harris's testimony at the subsequent trial, she entered Tarnower's bedroom, where he was sleeping, and she became enraged at the sight of her rival's nightgown. When Harris threw a box of curlers through the window, Tarnower awakened and slapped her. Harris later testified that she took out the gun, put it to her head, and pulled the trigger. Tarnower grabbed the gun; it went off and shot him in the hand. He went to the bathroom to wash his slight wound while Harris got the gun again.

As Tarnower tried to buzz for the housekeeper, he allegedly struggled with Harris over the gun and it went off, hitting Tarnower again. Harris then tried to shoot herself twice in the head, but the gun malfunctioned. However, the gun did shoot when she aimed it at the bed.

Harris could not reload the gun, so she later maintained that she smashed the weapon against the bathtub in anger. She also helped the bleeding doctor into bed and tried to call for help, but the phone did not work. Thinking the phone was out of order, Harris left the house to go to a nearby phone booth to call for help. When she returned, the housekeeper had called the police.

Harris was charged with second-degree murder. She had hoped that her story of attempted suicide and accidental death would be believed. However, the prosecution contended that Harris deliberately shot Tarnower. The first bullet went through his outstretched hand into his chest. Prosecutors contended that the second shot was also aimed deliberately and hit Tarnower in the shoulder. Harris and Tarnower struggled and the gun fired a wild bullet out the window. Another shot went into the bed. When Tarnower tried to call the housekeeper, the prosecution claimed Harris took dead aim and shot Tarnower in the arm.

At first, it was thought that four bullets had struck the victim. Later it was determined that one bullet had caused two injuries—one when it entered Tarnower's hand and again when it went into his chest.

Damaging testimony came from a medical expert who said that palm tissue was found in the chest wound. This proved that Tarnower had held up his hand in a futile defense attempt. The medical expert also testified that the chest wound was cylindrical, not round. The bullet apparently was "tumbling" when it struck his chest, the way it behaves after it strikes an intervening object.

The prosecution also read to the jury a long, bitter letter Harris had sent to Tarnower on the very day he died. The letter was full of rage against Tarnower's new lover. It seemed to provide a motive for the killing.

On February 5, 1981, Jean Harris was convicted of second-degree murder and sentenced to a minimum of 15 years to life.

BRUNO RICHARD HAUPTMANN
THE LINDBERGH BABY KIDNAPPER

THE AMERICAN PEOPLE REACTED TO THE KIDNAP-PING AS IF A BELOVED FAMILY MEMBER HAD BEEN ABDUCTED.

Other crimes have been more horrifying; other deeds have been bloodier; other felonies more skillfully executed. But no crime more completely took hold of an entire nation than the kidnapping of the Lindbergh baby.

When Charles A. Lindbergh flew his nonstop solo flight across the Atlantic in 1927, he was instantly transformed into a legendary hero. Handsome and possessed of a quiet courage and adventurous spirit, Lindbergh was adored by the public. Indeed, for many Americans Lindbergh embodied the best of the national character. When his son and only child was kidnapped and subsequently murdered, Americans felt a personal shock and grief over the tragedy that had befallen their idol.

It all started on the night of March 1, 1932, at the

Lindbergh country home outside Hopewell, New Jersey. At 9:00 P.M., Anne Morrow Lindbergh, wife of Charles Lindbergh, went up to the second floor nursery to check on their son, 20-month-old Charles Lindbergh, Jr. She found the child sleeping peacefully in his crib. At 9:50 P.M., the baby's nanny, Betty Gow, entered the nursery for a second check. This time the baby was missing. In his place a ransom note had been left on the windowsill, and an odd, home-built ladder lay on the ground near the side of the house.

At first, the question of who should be responsible for investigating the crime sparked a bitter jurisdictional dispute between the Hopewell police and the New Jersey state police. In the meantime, much important evidence was damaged or irretrievably lost. Once the investigation got underway, the police concentrated their efforts on a series of ransom notes the Lindberghs received from the unknown kidnapper. The police labored under an intense media scrutiny that went well beyond the bounds of good taste. Yet the media could claim with some justification that it was merely feeding the insatiable curiosity of the American people, who had reacted to the kidnapping as if a beloved family member had been abducted. A kind of hysteria was generated, one that pressured the police to make an arrest. The newspapers tripped over each other to report every morsel of fact or rumor no matter how intrusive, hurtful, or just plain false.

Lindbergh's meddling in the case presented a further hindrance to the police, as did the involvement of various individuals who thought they had a contribution to make. Among the latter were an heiress who offered to meet the kidnapper's ransom demands, and Chicago gangster Al Capone, who volunteered to help in any way he could—from his jail cell. Of more practical value were the efforts of the FBI, which was allowed to participate in the investigation after successfully lobbying Congress to pass the so-called Lindbergh Kidnapping Law.

Lengthy negotiations for a payout to the kidnapper were conducted by a certain Dr. John Condon, one of the many individuals who had made it their business to help Lindbergh. Dr. Condon met with a mysterious man in a cemetery who had enough information about the child to convince Lindbergh that he was genuine. On April 2, Lindbergh handed $50,000 in cash to Condon, who passed it on to the man. Condon was told where to pick up the child, but no one appeared at the given location. Lindbergh had been made the victim of a cruel, and expensive, hoax. But worse news was yet to come. On May 12, the badly decomposed body of Charles Lindbergh, Jr., was found in the woods not four miles from the family's New Jersey home.

With the discovery of the child's body, the entire nation entered a period of mourning. In addition to grief, another powerful emotion emerged from the public psyche: rage. Across the land a clamor for vengeance was raised on the Lindberghs' behalf. But vengeance had to wait some two and one-half years, until German immigrant Bruno Richard Hauptmann paid for gas at a Bronx service station with one of the marked bills from the ransom payoff. The attendant notified authorities, who immediately arrested Hauptmann. A search of the traveling carpenter's premises turned up more of the Lindbergh ransom money. It seemed the murderer had been found.

Or had he? Whether Hauptmann was the kidnapper/murderer of the Lindbergh baby remains a topic of controversy. Many criminal justice scholars maintain that the police and the prosecuting attorneys manufactured evidence that implicated Hauptmann, while at the same time they withheld evidence that might have exonerated him. Moreover, it is known that many prosection witnesses lied on the stand or were coached about what to say. Yet legal malpractice does not an innocent man make, and there remains a strong possibility that Hauptmann was indeed the killer of Charles Lindbergh's son.

Innocent or guilty, Hauptmann was indicted for the crime. His 1935 trial was conducted openly, amidst heavy media coverage. A circus atmosphere prevailed in the courtroom, where radio broadcasters and newsreel cameramen were in constant and clamorous attendance. In the end, Hauptmann was found guilty and sentenced to die in the electric chair. Shortly before his scheduled execution, the Governor of New Jersey offered to commute his sentence to life imprisonment in exchange for an admission of guilt. Hauptmann refused, and was duly put to death on April 3, 1936. His willingness to die is as puzzling as the question of his guilt. Was this his way of punishing himself for a crime he had committed—or was it the last prideful act of an innocent man?

NEVILLE HEATH

AN OFFICER AND A GENTLEMAN WITH MURDER ON HIS MIND AND A WHIP IN HIS HAND.

The rubble from Nazi air raids could still be seen on some London streets on June 21, 1946, when the discovery of a disfigured body in a hotel room shocked the city. A young woman was found dead in a room in London's Pembridge Court Hotel. She had been suffocated, but more shocking was the clear evidence that she had been whipped and then badly mutilated.

Mr. and Mrs. N.G.C. Heath had checked into the room at the Pembridge Court five days earlier, according to the hotel's registry. Neville George Clevely Heath was a handsome 29-year-old who had served as a Royal Air Force bomber pilot during the war. The woman registered at the hotel as his wife, who became the victim of his vicious attack, was 32-year-old Margery Gardner. She had worked as an extra in motion pictures. The evening before her body was discovered, Margery and Heath had been seen together drinking and dancing at the Panama Club, a hot London night spot.

As soon as the murder was discovered, the police began searching for Heath. From the beginning he was the prime suspect.

Heath had gotten out of London and was traveling around the English coast. He ended up in Bournemouth, where he checked into a room at the Tollard Royal Hotel using the name Captain Rupert Brooke. Why Heath chose as an alias the name of the well-known and beloved poet whose poems about World War I were memorized by every English schoolboy remains a mystery.

Not long after Heath arrived in the area, a young woman who was visiting Bournemouth disappeared. When Miss Doreen Marshall failed to return to her room at the Norfolk Hotel after several days, authorities grew suspicious. The manager of Heath's hotel mentioned to him that inquiries were being made about the young woman. Doreen and Heath had dined together a few days earlier. Heath told his hotel's manager that he was going to offer his assistance to the local police in their search for the missing woman.

When he entered the Bournemouth police station on June 28, Heath had no idea that the police there had a complete description and photograph of him. They immediately arrested him on suspicion of murder. Heath remained cool and insisted he was Rupert Brooke. The police found Heath's whip and his other hideous paraphernalia, and two days after he was taken into custody, Doreen Marshall's body was found. She also had been violently assaulted.

During their investigation, the police discovered that Neville Heath, a former RAF officer, had been shot down in May 1944 while piloting a bomber. During his short life, Heath had been in trouble repeatedly, but he had no record of violent crime. Most of his offenses occurred while he was in the military. But the reason Heath developed a violent personality remains unclear.

At his trial, Heath entered a plea of insanity. The jury rejected his defense and after a brief deliberation returned a guilty verdict. Heath was executed on October 16, 1946.

GARY HEIDNIK

SIX WOMEN HELD PRISONER IN A "HOUSE OF HORRORS" IN PHILADELPHIA WERE TORTURED AND RAPED—TWO DID NOT SURVIVE.

Weak and in a state of dehydration and semistarvation, Josephina Rivera, 26, escaped from Gary Heidnik and ran for the police. On March 25, 1987, she led police to Heidnik's run-down Philadelphia row house, where three other women were held captive in a damp basement. Lisa Thomas, 19, and Agnes Adams, 24, were chained to pipes, and Jacqueline Askins, 18, was found alive in a stench-filled basement pit that had been covered with plywood. Police also found 24 pounds of frozen limbs in his refrigerator believed to be the remains of 24-year-old Sandra Lindsay.

Rivera said she had been captive since November 1986; the other three had come in ensuing months. The women had been repeatedly raped, beaten, and given electric shocks. One report states that Heidnik had jammed a screwdriver into one victim's ears. Heidnik had also manipulated his captives psychologically, pitting one woman against the other by encouraging them to inform on each other's disobedience. Heidnik had told his captives he planned to capture ten prisoners to father his children.

The four surviving victims, held captive in the house during Heidnik's murderous spree, said Lindsay was hung from a ceiling beam for several days until she was dead. Heidnik then cut up her body in the basement with an electric saw. He reportedly bragged to the survivors he was feeding them parts of Lindsay's body.

Rivera also led police to a state forest in New Jersey, where they found the body of a second woman, 23-year-old Deborah Dudley. Testimony during Heidnik's trial revealed that he electrocuted Dudley while she stood in a water-filled pit in his basement. Heidnik touched live electrical wires to her chains. He then dumped her body in the Wharton State Forest.

Heidnik had a history of deviant sexual behavior and violent outbursts. In the late 1960s, he was known to hang around an institute for retarded people; he lured young black and Hispanic women clients to his house for sex. Complaints were never followed up by authorities. In the early 1970s, he formed the United Church of the Ministries of God and ordained himself a bishop. The tiny congregation reportedly consisted only of people from the institute for retarded people. In 1976, he shot a disgruntled tenant in an apartment building he owned. The wound was superficial, and charges were dropped. In 1978, he received a prison term of three to seven years for kidnapping and raping a 34-year-old retarded woman from a Harrisburg institution. The woman was the sister of Heidnik's girlfriend at the time. He served four years and four months. After he moved to the Philadelphia house, neighbors complained about smells of burning flesh and sounds of electric saws in the middle of the night, but their concerns were dismissed.

In July 1988, Heidnik was convicted of first-degree murder, kidnapping, rape, aggravated assault, and involuntary deviate sexual intercourse in the Philadelphia case. He showed no emotion as his conviction was read. Jurors rejected an insanity defense and sentenced him to death. In late 1988, he attempted suicide by poisoning himself and slipped into a coma.

THE HERNANDEZ BROTHERS AND MAGDALENA SOLIS

"HIGH PRIEST" SANTOS HERNANDEZ SEXUALLY "PURI-FIED" A TEENAGE GIRL. WATCHING THE INTIMACIES STIMULATED MAGDALENA SOLIS'S DESIRES FOR HER.

The peasants in the Mexican village of Yerba Buena still feared the old Inca gods of the mountains. In 1963, the brothers Santos and Cayetano Hernandez devised a scheme to make money by taking advantage of these fears. They convinced the villagers that they could acquire gems and gold if they worshipped those Inca gods and made sacrifices to them. They talked the villagers into "donating" their money and most of their earthly possessions. To provide an atmosphere of ritualistic extravagance, they brought in a lesbian prostitute, Magdalena Solis, and her homosexual brother, Eleazor, to participate in the sinister rites.

In the center of the cultic service, which was held in a mountain cave, a brazier of hot coals cast a subtle glow. Flash powder thrown on the embers brought forth clouds of smoke. As the smoke cleared, Magdalena and Eleazor "magically" appeared. The peasants, told by the Hernandez brothers that Eleazor was St. Francis of Assisi, immediately acknowledged him as this saint. This "miracle" caused a frenzied reaction among the peasants, who beat and hacked away at the mountainside.

In the midst of this spirited emotional contagion, "High Priest" Santos Hernandez sexually "purified" a teenage girl, Celina Salvana. Magdalena Solis watched the intimacies between Santos and Celina, which stimulated her own desires for the girl. Santos then passed the young Celina to Magdalena. Meanwhile, Eleazor Solis and Cayetano Hernandez, who preferred males, took advantage of the boys in the assemblage.

But one skeptical villager, Jesus Rubio, doubted the sanctity of the Hernandez brothers. Challenged, they took Rubio into their confidence and paid him off with a share of the take. As the rituals began to get out of control, the peasants started to complain that the promised Inca treasures were not appearing. In an effort to quell the peasants' objections, Magdalena preached the requirements of "sacrifice" that the gods demanded. She revealed that only by cleansing out disbelievers could the jewels of the gods be delivered.

Two men who had refused to accept the word of

the Inca gods were quickly beaten to death. The victims' blood was mixed with that of a chicken and drunk from a sacrificial bowl by the assemblage. During the following two months, six more disbelievers were killed in the continuing ritual gatherings. Many others fled in fright.

During this time, Celina craved Santos more and more, touching off a jealous rage in Magdalena, who had the girl bound to a sacrificial cross. In a "spiritual offering" of her own, Magdalena beat the teenage girl unconscious. The spellbound peasantry continued the pummeling until Celina was dead. A passing student, Sebastian Gurrero, witnessed the final stage of this ordeal: The worshipers piled brush around Celina's body and set it afire.

In terror, Gurrero rushed to the police station in the village of Villa Gran and reported what he had seen. Patrolman Luis Martinez reluctantly agreed to drive the boy back to Yerba Buena. They were never seen alive again; their mutilated bodies were discovered during the police follow-up.

Santos Hernandez was killed in a shoot-out with police, but Cayetano Hernandez disappeared. Jesus Rubio later confessed that he had killed Cayetano so he could be "High Priest." In June 1963, Magdalena Solis, Eleazor, and 12 cult members were tried, convicted, and sent to prison for 30 years.

RICHARD HICKOCK AND PERRY SMITH

NO PLACE, IT SEEMED, WAS SAFE FROM SENSELESS VIOLENCE.

A crime so brutal that it shocked the nation was committed by two small-time thugs who probably could not have gone through with their plan if either of them had been acting alone. But ex-convicts Richard Hickock and Perry Smith each seemed to bring out the other's worst impulses. Their story is one of greed, violence, and above all, stupidity.

A former cellmate, Floyd Wells, had once worked for Herbert W. Clutter, a prosperous farmer in Holcomb, Kansas. Some of Wells's remarks led Hickock and Smith to believe that Clutter kept large sums of cash in the house. The dim-witted duo wasted little time in starting to plan their big heist.

Like every other crook, they were motivated by a dream of personal gain, but their dream was unusual: The pair planned to use their booty to retire to an island off the coast of South America, where they planned on diving for hidden treasure.

Shortly past midnight on November 15, 1959, the pair entered the Clutter home through an unlocked side door. They confronted Herbert Clutter in his bedroom and kept him at bay with a hunting knife. Floyd Wells had told Hickock and Smith that the Clutter cash was kept in a hidden safe. They demanded to be told the safe's whereabouts, but Clutter answered that the only money in the house was the $30 in his wallet.

Hickock and Smith didn't believe Clutter. The terrified farmer was forced to wake his wife, Bonnie, who burst into tears and said, "I don't have any money." The group then awakened the Clutter's 15-year-old son, Kenyon. Sixteen-year-old Nancy Clutter came to investigate the noise, and was promptly tied up. Hickock liked Nancy's looks and was on the verge of raping her when Smith told him to forget about the idea. Momentarily at a loss and unsure of what to do next, the pair concluded the break-in by using a shotgun and the knife to kill the entire Clutter family.

When the bodies were discovered the next day, a shock wave of anger and fear swept across the American heartland. No place, it seemed, was safe from senseless violence. The local public outcry was tremendous, and a large police investigation was organized in response to it.

When the imprisoned Floyd Wells heard about the murders, he contacted the authorities and told them what he knew. The two killers were subsequently tracked to Las Vegas and apprehended. Once separated, each informed on the other without hesitation.

The investigation and trial relating to this sensational, highly publicized case consumed nearly four years. In the end, Richard Hickock and Perry Smith were found guilty. They were hanged on April 14, 1965.

While the trial was underway, noted author Truman Capote became fascinated by the case and was able to interest *The New Yorker* in an article. Capote traveled to Kansas and interviewed the two condemned men extensively before their executions. His research produced the best-selling book, *In Cold Blood*, which in turn inspired a well-received 1967 motion picture of the same title. Hickock and Smith had made their mark, but they would be remembered only as two of the most savage and stupid criminals who ever lived.

THE HILLSIDE STRANGLER
ANGELO BUONO AND KENNETH BIANCHI

IN A SPARE BEDROOM, WHICH THEY CALLED "THE TORTURE CHAMBER," THE COUSINS RAPED AND BRUTALIZED THEIR VICTIMS BEFORE KILLING THEM.

For half a year, from October 1977 to February 1978, the women of Los Angeles lived in terror of the Hillside Strangler—a vicious killer (or killers) who discarded his tortured victims in the hills around the sprawling metropolitan area. By the time the L.A. killings stopped, ten young women were dead and the police had no suspects. But the murder spree was not over; it had merely moved. Eleven months later, the Hillside Strangler struck again in Bellingham, Washington. The disappearance and death of two young college women eventually lead police to Kenneth Bianchi.

Along with his cousin Angelo Buono, Bianchi was the Hillside Strangler. Between them, the cousins brutally tortured and killed 12 young women. Both men were born in Rochester, New York. Buono moved to Glendale, California, near

Los Angeles and started an upholstery business. Bianchi, who is 15 years younger than his cousin, moved to California in 1975. Within two years, the men had taken up their ghoulish pastime.

The young women they raped and then murdered ranged in age from 12 to 28 years old. With the exception of the final victims who were found in the trunk of a car that had been pushed over a cliff, the men dumped the bodies of their victims along rural roads.

Curiously, neither Buono nor Bianchi had a background of violent crime. Perhaps they were motivated by some warped spirit of adventure. Maybe they merely wanted to experience the thrill of killing someone. In any event, they found homicide to their liking.

They agreed from the outset that working as a team would make the murders easier to commit. Buono often posed as a policeman to gain the trust of the intended victims, whereupon they were abducted and driven to his house. The hapless females were taken to a spare bedroom, appropriately dubbed "the torture chamber," and strapped into a chair. Then the victims were raped repeatedly, penetrated with various instruments, and finally strangled to death.

Each successive victim, it seemed, was subjected to even more unthinkable horrors than the previous one. One young woman was injected with a cleaning fluid, then gassed to death with a bag that had been placed over her head and connected to the oven with a hose. Another helpless victim was subjected to electric shock torture before being strangled.

Ten murders were committed in Los Angeles before the killings came to an abrupt halt in February 1978. Homicide detectives were convinced that the murders were the work of two men, but had no firm suspects and little in the way of evidence. Spurred on by harsh public criticism of their efforts, the police labored long and hard to solve the case. Privately, though, many investigators doubted that the killers would ever be caught.

On January 11, 1979, the baffled Los Angeles police got an unexpected break. Two female students in Bellingham, Washington, disappeared from the house they shared. Their bodies were found the next day in the trunk of the car belonging to one of them. This discovery prompted a friend of one victim to come forward. Recently, the friend said, the murdered girl had mentioned something about a "surveillance" job that a security guard had offered her. The guard's name was Kenneth Bianchi, and he had recently moved to Bellingham from Los Angeles.

Questioned by local police, Bianchi initially denied any involvement in the Bellingham murders. He changed his story when confronted with irrefutable evidence found at the murder scene, plus statements from witnesses. Astute lawmen quickly concluded that they had cracked California's Hillside Strangler case as well.

Hoping to cut a deal with the authorities, Bianchi implicated his cousin in the Hillside Strangler killings. Bianchi admitted to the murder of five Hillside Strangler victims and testified against Angelo Buono. As a result, Buono was convicted of nine murders and sentenced to a life term without the possibility of parole. Bianchi was sentenced to life imprisonment in Washington State; he must serve a minimum term of 26 2/3 years before receiving his first parole hearing.

JOHANN OTTO HOCH

MARRYING MONEY WAS THE NAME OF THE GAME FOR THIS CHICAGO BLUEBEARD.

Marriage drives some people to murder. Johann Otto Hoch married to murder. This mild-mannered Chicago meat packer wed 24 women in 14 years. He walked out on the lucky ones, leaving them penniless. He murdered the unlucky ones as soon as he had taken control of their finances.

Hoch emigrated to Chicago in the 1880s. His real name was John Schmidt, and he was born in Germany in 1862. Like many German immigrants in the Windy City, he worked in the meat-packing industry, expecting to grow rich in America. But his job was tough and unpleasant, and for an ambitious man like Hoch, the work was no way to get ahead.

In 1892 he began to place advertisements in lonely hearts columns. "Gentleman. . . wishes acquaintance of widow . . . object matrimony," his ads read. When the responses came in, he graded them strictly on the basis of the respondent's wealth. Only rich widows took his fancy. After a whirlwind courtship, Hoch would gain control of his new wife's assets. Never one to hang around, Hoch would disappear soon after he was in possession of his spouse's valuables. If he didn't beat a quick retreat, he would extricate himself from the marriage by poisoning his new wife.

Hoch's last two wives were Marie Walcker and her sister, Amelia. When Marie died within a month of the wedding, Hoch proposed to Amelia. When she criticized him about a period of mourning, Hoch told her, "The dead are for the dead, the living for the living." Amelia and Hoch were married, and within days, he vanished with all her money. The puzzled, grieving, angry newlywed went to the police. The death of Marie within a month and the abandonment of Amelia were coincidences too great for the police to ignore.

In January 1905, the police were able to piece together a pattern of dead or defrauded women. Word went out to be on the lookout for Hoch. A New York landlady named Katherine Kimmerle complained that her new tenant looked like Hoch and had proposed marriage to her.

After his arrest, Hoch denied everything, and he even claimed that they had the wrong Hoch. Among his possessions was a fountain pen containing arsenic, traces of which were found in the exhumed Marie Walcker. Johann Otto Hoch was found guilty in Chicago and hanged on February 23, 1906.

JAMES OLIVER HUBERTY

HE TOLD HIS WIFE THAT HE PLANNED TO GO "HUNTING FOR HUMANS." SHE HAD NO IDEA HER DISTURBED HUSBAND WAS DEAD SERIOUS.

The Massillon, Ohio, plant where James Oliver Huberty worked closed down in 1983, and he lost his job. He was 41 years old and faced a crisis. He decided he would be better able to find a job in the thriving economy of California. In December 1983, the Huberty family moved to San Ysidro, a suburb of San Diego just north of the Mexican border. Huberty intended to make a new beginning in a new location.

Huberty found a job as a security guard, but he was soon fired. Frustrated and unhappy, Huberty didn't know where to turn. He felt the move to California had been his last chance.

On July 18, 1984, an angry-at-the-world Huberty left home carrying a rifle, pistol, shotgun, and a great deal of ammunition. He told his wife that he planned to go "hunting for humans." She had no idea her disturbed husband was dead serious.

Huberty didn't go far for the hunt. The local McDonald's restaurant was close to his home. Huberty began shooting indiscriminately, aiming his fire furiously both inside and outside the crowded restaurant. In no time at all, 21 people died, and 19 were wounded in the attack. Most of the victims were children. It was one of the largest mass shootings by an individual on record. Huberty died when he was struck by a hail of bullets from the hastily summoned SWAT team.

CHARLES JONES

ENTANGLED IN A VILE CONSPIRACY OF GREED, CHARLES JONES MURDERED HIS EMPLOYER, THE WEALTHY MAN HE VOWED TO SERVE.

Charles Jones made a career serving others. As the personal secretary and manservant of William Marsh Rice, a self-made multimillionaire, Jones was a trusted and faithful companion. But what turned this man against his employer was an all-consuming greed.

Rice moved into the rich territory of Texas in the early 1830s. Speculating in oil and land, creating store and hotel chains, he was a much-admired multimillionaire by the turn of the century. He intended to return his wealth to the land that had given him his fortune through a nonprofit public works corporation he wanted set up after his death and call the Rice Institute. He was living out his final days in luxury in New York City, with his trusted friend Charles Jones.

Albert Patrick, a roguish lawyer at best, endeared himself to Charles Jones while employed by relatives of Rice's late wife to free up some of Mr. Rice's fortune for themselves. Patrick initially sought Jones's help in winning the lawsuit. However, when he discerned Jones's willingness to engage in some deceit, Patrick forgot about his clients. Jones gave Patrick access to all of Rice's personal papers, checks, will, and other legal documents. From March to September of 1900, they built a paper trail suggesting that Patrick had become Rice's lawyer and friend. A new will was written (leaving 90 percent of his fortune to Patrick), as were a power of attorney and checks totaling $250,000.

Jones persuaded Rice to switch to a new physician, Walter Curry. Dr. Curry had no part in the conspiracy, but the aged doctor's failing eyesight and faulty memory made him the ideal dupe. Jones began to give mercury tablets to Rice, which created digestive trouble that Dr. Curry began to treat. On September 23, 1900, on Patrick's instructions, Jones administered a lethal dose of chloroform to the sleeping Rice. Waiting long enough for the telltale odor to subside, Jones called the physician. Dr. Curry signed the death certificate, which read "Cause of death—old age and a weak heart; immediate causes—indigestion followed by collacratal diarrhoea with mental worry."

Patrick sent Rice's body for cremation. If he'd waited until that was completed, there would have been only Dr. Curry's certificate for evidence. However, he was too eager and immediately presented the Swenson banking house with a forged check for $25,000. Patrick misspelled his name on the check to cover up the fact that he made it out to himself. This prompted the bankers' initial suspicion. Although the bankers did not doubt the check's authenticity, they decided to check with Mr. Rice before handing out such a sum to a stranger. When they called Rice's residence, Charles Jones was obliged to tell them that Rice was dead and about to be cremated. The alarmed bankers called the police and district attorney. The cremation was stayed and an autopsy ordered, which showed the deadly gas in Rice's lungs.

Jones was granted limited immunity in exchange for testifying against the person that the authorities felt was primarily responsible for Rice's death—Patrick. The sensational month-long trial featured charges and countercharges. Medical experts attacked each other's opinions, and handwriting specialists likewise feuded. Patrick was found guilty of first-degree murder on March 26, 1902, and sentenced to die in the electric chair. However, he fought on legally for ten years. On November 28, 1912, he was pardoned.

Today, Rice University—endowed by Mr. Rice's millions—is one of the finest institutions of higher learning in the South.

JIM JONES

912 INNOCENT PEOPLE DIED OF POISON IN GUYANA'S JUNGLES AS REVEREND JIM JONES PLAYED GOD.

The Reverend Jim Jones possessed more than charisma when he first began his own ministry in Indianapolis, Indiana, in the late 1950s. He claimed to have healing powers. Maintaining that he was part of the Christian Church sect, the Disciples of Christ, Jones organized his interracial followers into what he called his "People's Temple."

Jones's psychological hold over his followers was uncanny. He had absolutely no problem finding people to join his sect—after all, there are many people in this world who are searching for happiness and are willing to follow a seemingly genuine leader. Once Jones got people to join his ministry, however, he exerted a progressively firmer grasp on them. He persuaded his new followers to turn over their money and possessions to the Temple by convincing them that their acts would help build a better world.

Unaware that they were blindly serving a ranting and raving maniac, there was no question that Jones's followers meant well. They performed deeds time and again that benefitted mankind. His followers were dedicated to integration and concerned with all the things that they felt mattered in life.

Although his People's Temple ministry received a great deal of praise, Jones eventually became dissatisfied. He wanted more power, wealth, and recognition to feed his already bloated ego. Hoping to achieve those ends and build his ministry to a national level, he moved to Ukiah, California, in the mid-1960s. About 150 people followed him.

Despite Jones's secrecy-induced paranoia and unchecked obsessiveness, the People's Temple grew and prospered. By the early 1970s, the cult had established firm roots in Los Angeles and San Francisco. Jones's presentations of supposed healings continued to bring in new members, most of whom he quickly dominated by demanding total selflessness in return for his assurances of a better life and a better world.

Because Jones and his sect were so secretive, little information about their activities was shared with nonmembers. However, by the mid-1970s, members began to defect, and the stories they told generated serious questions about the People's Temple.

Defectors revealed that Jones's healings were dramatically staged and completely fraudulent. Reports of beatings, mysterious deaths, and deviant sexual practices within the cult also began to surface. Faced with increasing pressure from journalists and law enforcement organizations, Jones began looking for a way out.

He soon found what he believed would be his salvation in Guyana, a small former British colony on the northeast coast of South America. Much of the country, which is about the size of the state of Idaho, is undeveloped and difficult to reach; that appealed to Jones immensely. In 1975, he founded Jonestown in an outlying region of the country, and the majority of the People's Temple settlers moved to the remote site that same year.

Pressured by increasing speculation and investigations in the United States, Jones virtually shut down his San Francisco and Los Angeles operations in May 1977 after convincing nearly 1,000 members of his People's Temple to move to Jonestown. After wrapping up the loose ends, Jones left for Guyana in August 1977.

The Jonestown project cost the People's Temple "investors" an estimated five million dollars. However, it soon became a fully functional community, complete with generators for electricity, tractors for farming, and buildings to house livestock. Cult members also built classrooms in which to teach their children. Given a less deranged leader, the community might have flourished.

However, over the next year, Jones's behavior changed dramatically for the worse. He became more domineering, and he began to subject cult members to more stringent discipline and regimentation, demanding total personal submission to his authority. Jones implemented programs that entailed psychological pressures and brainwashing, forced labor, and physical abuse that bordered on torture. In short, he had turned Jonestown into a concentration camp.

There was strong evidence to suggest that Jones began abusing drugs during his final year, and he might have developed a psychosis. In his sermons from the Jonestown pavilion, which were nothing more than emotional sessions he termed "white nights," Jones began to dishonor the Bible and deny the power of God. Instead of preaching the gospel, he dwelled on sex, revolution, defectors, external and internal enemies, and death and suicide. Some said that he began to hallucinate and that he eventually came to believe he was God.

There were, naturally, a number of defections. Viewing the defectors as traitors to his cause, Jones's anger soon turned to rage. Eventually, reports that members of the People's Temple were being held against their will reached the United States. Those reports were brought to the attention of a Northern California congressman.

On November 17, 1978, Representative Leo Ryan brought a group of American journalists and relatives of temple members to Jonestown to observe first-hand the conditions there. Although alarmed by what he saw, Ryan spent the night in Jonestown.

Tension was high the next morning, November 18, as Ryan and his delegation left for an airstrip seven miles away. Several Jonestown residents had declared that they wanted to return to the United States, but an angry Jones denied their right to leave. After declaring that a conspiracy was underway to destroy his organization, Jones sent a death squad to the airstrip.

Armed with automatic weapons, the death squad opened fire on Congressman Ryan, members of his staff, journalists, and relatives of cult members as they walked toward the waiting airplane. When the shooting was over, Ryan and four other people were dead. Ten others were seriously wounded.

Back at Jonestown, Jones assembled everyone at the pavilion and told them that their community would soon be attacked. He insisted that everyone had to "take the potion like they used to take in ancient Greece." It turned out that the potion consisted of a lethal mixture of grape Kool-Aid and potassium cyanide.

The potion was mixed in a large metal tub and placed in the pavilion. Jones, promising that they were "going to meet again in another place," ordered that infants go first. Volunteers dutifully used syringes to squirt the poison into the backs of the crying children's mouths.

Paper cups filled with the deadly drink were then passed out to the adults and older children. Those who resisted were injected as armed guards stood by, ready to shoot anyone who disobeyed Jones's orders. Everyone else drank the potion, some enthusiastically. Most were dead within five minutes. A few lucky people managed to flee into the jungle and lived to tell about the tragedy.

Satisfied that he had brought his cult to "a gallant, glorious, screaming end," Jones, it is believed, shot a close aide to death moments before taking his own life by firing a single bullet from a .38-caliber pistol into his brain. When it was over, 912 followers of the People's Temple cult and their leader lay dead on and around the Jonestown pavilion. The bodies of men, women, and children covered the ground. Some were holding hands; some were clutching each other in a death embrace. It was a scene that shocked the world, created by a man who played God to show everyone that he was in control, even at the end.

STEVEN JUDY

HIS HISTORY OF SEX CRIMES STARTED WHEN HE WAS ONLY TEN YEARS OLD.

When the American Civil Liberties Union tried to prevent the execution of Steven T. Judy, 24, for the 1979 strangulation and rape of Terry Chasteen and the murder of her three children, Misty Ann, 5, Stephen Michael, 4, and Mark Lewis, 2, Judy told the judge, "They're actually doing it against my will."

Judy's chance encounter with Chasteen occurred just five days after he had been released on bond where he was awaiting trial on armed robbery charges. He had been bailed out by his foster father, Bob Carr.

He was driving along Interstate 465 near Indianapolis when he pulled along side Chasteen's car. He signaled to her that something was wrong with her car. They both pulled to the side of the road. When he raised her hood, he was able to pull out an ignition wire, preventing the car from starting again.

Judy offered Chasteen and her children a ride.

Once they were in the car, he drove them to White Lick Creek. There he forced Chasteen to undress and raped her. The children, who were some feet away, came running back to the scene. Judy then strangled her with the gag he had been using during the rape and threw her—and then the children—into the creek.

This was not Judy's first sex crime. When he was only ten years old, he was arrested for knocking a woman down and squeezing her breasts. At age 13 he knocked on a woman's door, posing as a Boy Scout. She let him inside, where he raped her and repeatedly stabbed her with a knife until the blade broke. He went into the kitchen to get another knife, and when he returned, he found her with a hatchet she was trying to use for protection. He took that from her and hit her on the head.

However, the woman was not killed. After brain surgery and open-heart surgery, she recovered. Judy was committed to Central State Hospital Mental Institution in Indianapolis. His foster parents, Bob and Mary Carr, met him there; Judy had become friends with Carr's half-brother, Tony Colvin. For the next 11 years, Judy spent 75 percent of his life in either a jail or a mental institution. When he was free, he lived with the Carrs.

During his trial for the murder of Chasteen and her children, a state psychologist testified that Judy was legally insane at the time of the murders, calling him a psychopath. Judy was convicted of the murders in February of 1980 and was sentenced to death. At the time he agreed to an appeal.

But when it looked as if he might have to spend his entire life in prison, he told his lawyer to stop the appeal. He said he'd rather be executed than live in prison, calling prison unbearable.

Judy was executed by the state of Indiana at 12:12 A.M., March 9, 1981, the first person executed in Indiana since 1961.

PATRICK KEARNEY

YOUNG, HOMOSEXUAL MEN WERE SHOT, DISMEMBERED, AND STUFFED IN PLASTIC TRASH BAGS.

When Patrick Kearney and David Hill walked into the Riverside, California, police station on July 1, 1977, and identified the wanted poster on the wall saying "That's us," police were finally able to close the chapter on what at the time could have been the largest mass murder investigation in the nation's history.

Kearney and Hill were wanted in connection with the gruesome "trash bag murders," which included at least 28 victims—possibly as many as 40—between the years of 1968 and 1977. Most of the victims were homosexuals and were found nude. The victims were shot and several were dismembered with either a knife or a hacksaw. The remains of each victim were stuffed in a plastic trash bag. The bags were left at various locations from Los Angeles south to the Mexican border.

Kearney, 37, and Hill, 34, were homosexuals who had moved to California in 1967 shortly after Hill divorced his wife. They had lived together for about 15 years, most recently in an apartment in Redondo Beach, a suburb of Los Angeles. When Kearney recounted his tale for police, he said it was just one year after the move that he claimed his first victim, identified only as George, and buried him behind his duplex in Culver City.

But the trash bag murders might have started in April 1975, possibly with the deaths of several other victims. Police found the body of 21-year-old Albert Rivera near San Juan Capistrano. Soon more bodies turned up. All victims were shot in the head; some were partially dismembered, and all left in plastic bags. By March 1977, the body count had risen to eight, all showing the same pattern.

The final victim, 17-year-old John LaMay, disappeared March 13 after he said he was going to visit his friend Dave. When his partially dismembered body was found five days later, police recognized it as another trash bag murder. But this case was different.

Most of Kearney's victims were hitchhikers or male prostitutes picked up at random. LaMay had set out to visit his killer. The young man's friends told police that "Dave" was David Hill, and they could even supply his address.

When the investigation focused on the homosexual lovers in May 1977, Kearney, who was known as a gifted electronics engineer, quit his job at Hughes Aircraft Corporation. While evidence taken during a search of the men's residence were being analyzed, the duo fled.

Inside their apartment police found a hacksaw stained with blood from one of the victims, bloodstains from a victim, strands of a victim's hair, tape similar to that found binding a victim's hands, and the material from a plastic bag used to dispose of a victim.

When Kearney and Hill turned themselves in, police were searching for both suspects. But Kearney's story was that he alone killed the men and boys because "it excited him and gave him a feeling of dominance." A grand jury later ruled there was insufficient evidence to implicate Hill and he was released.

Kearney then began leading police through his life of crime, and most of the information police ascertained about the trash bag murders came from Kearney himself. Almost ten years after Kearney's first murder, police dug up the remains of "George." Kearney also led investigators to other burial sites.

In all, Kearney signed 28 confessions. He eventually was given two sentences of life in prison for 12 confirmed murders. Police said in many other cases Kearney probably did commit the murder, but gathering evidence would be difficult after the bodies had spent so much time decomposing in the desert heat.

EDMUND KEMPER

"CURED" AFTER SPENDING TIME IN A PSYCHIATRIC HOSPITAL, KEMPER KILLED, RAPED, AND MUTILATED EIGHT WOMEN.

The case of mass murderer Edmund Kemper threw the mental health system of Santa Cruz, California, into a state of turmoil. Before he was convicted of murdering eight women in the early 1970s, most of them university students, he spent five years in a mental institution for killing his grandparents at age 14. He was deemed "cured" in 1969, and the California Youth Authority, responsible for juvenile offenders, took charge of him for the next three years. He was freed in 1972.

Kemper's grisly murders after his release included the decapitation of his victims, which he performed with a large hunting knife he called "the General." In addition, he performed sexual acts with the cadavers.

Kemper demonstrated sadistic behavior at an early age. He once reportedly cut the hands and head off his sister's doll; he carved up the family cat at the age of 10. He also reportedly had fantasies of killing his mother, Clarenell Strandberg, with whom he frequently quarrelled.

Kemper's parents divorced when he was seven. At 13, he ran away to live with his father, because he felt his mother ridiculed him. He eventually was sent to live with his father's parents on their North Fork, California, ranch. Strandberg, apparently concerned about her son's sadistic behavior, called her ex-husband to warn him that his parents might be in danger.

Her fears were realized. After arguing with his grandmother in August of 1963, Kemper shot her in the back of the head with a rifle; he stabbed her multiple times after she was dead. He shot his grandfather outside the house and then telephoned his mother and the local sheriff to confess. After eight years in a mental institution and youth detention, Kemper was pronounced "cured" and returned to live with his mother. However, his hatred for her did not subside over the years, and they had frequent, violent arguments.

His coed murdering spree began in May of 1972 with the deaths of Anita Luchessa and Mary Ann Pesce, both students at Fresno State College. The six-foot-nine-inch, 300-pound Kemper ordered Luchessa into the trunk of his car at gunpoint in a secluded spot. He then handcuffed Pesce, placed a plastic bag over her head, and stabbed her several times in the back and stomach. He then stabbed Luchessa to death. He took the corpses home and cut them up while his mother was out. He buried them in the mountains.

In September, he killed a 15-year-old female hitchhiker, performed sexual acts with the corpse, and carved up the body in his apartment. He buried the remains. In January of 1973, he picked up another hitchhiker, shot her, dissected the body at home, and threw the pieces over the cliffs near Carmel. In February, he shot two more women and carved up their bodies. His mother was home, so Kemper had to wait until the next morning to have sex with the corpses and to dissect them.

On Easter Sunday, he carried out his sadistic fantasy with his mother. He bludgeoned her with a hammer, decapitated the corpse, and hauled the remains to a closet. He then strangled his mother's friend who stopped by to visit. The next day, he drove off to Pueblo, Colorado. Three days later, he called the Santa Cruz police and confessed, saying he might kill again.

Kemper made a detailed confession and admitted cutting pieces of hair and skin from his victims and keeping them as trophies. He reportedly had an IQ of 131 and was found to be legally sane; he was sentenced to life in prison.

PETER KURTEN

KURTEN NOT ONLY RELISHED THE ACT OF MURDER; HE LIKED TO DRINK THE BLOOD OF HIS VICTIMS.

The German city of Düsseldorf was engulfed with fear during the summer of 1929. A madman, a homicidal maniac, was attacking young women and molesting, raping, and murdering them. Even little girls were not safe. In a single day—August 23—the unknown slayer killed a five-year-old girl and a 14-year-old girl, and he attempted to rape a 26-year-old woman. These random acts of violence created an atmosphere of terror that pervaded the city. Parents, hysterical with fear for their daughters, kept their children close to home. Strangers were regarded with distrust, and even close friends became suspicious. The city called the killer the Vampire of Düsseldorf. Some ten years later, the German filmmaker Fritz Lang captured the paranoic mood of the city in his classic thriller *M*, which was based on the episode of the Vampire.

A newcomer to Düsseldorf, Maria Budlick, finally led to the capture of the Vampire. When she arrived by train on the night of May 14, 1930, a man near the station offered to show her the way to a hostel for young women. Having heard of the Vampire of Düsseldorf, Budlick was distrustful and tried to avoid going with him. The man started a loud, angry argument with Budlick. Another man appeared and rescued Budlick by sending the first man away.

This second man, kindly and middle-aged, seemed quite harmless. Budlick accepted his offer to feed her dinner at his apartment. After eating, the man offered to escort her to the women's hostel. On the way, her supposed benefactor pulled her into a forest preserve and sexually assaulted her. The hapless woman struggled to no avail. She was on the verge of passing out when the man grabbed her by the throat and asked if she remembered where he lived. She told him she didn't, and he let her go.

But Maria Budlick had lied. The next day she led the police to his apartment. His name was Peter Kurten, and he knew that the police were watching him. Certain that the jig was just about up, he told his wife that he was the Vampire of Düsseldorf. On May 24, Kurten's wife reported this to the police, who picked him up that same day.

Kurten cooperated fully, providing a complete account of his terrible deeds. His trial began on April 13, 1931. Thousands of spectators crowded into a converted gymnasium. They were amazed to discover that the Vampire of Düsseldorf was a bland 48-year-old man with polite manners and meticulous habits. He seemed incapable of violence.

Yet violence was indeed his specialty. This he revealed in detail during his trial. In a low, monotone voice, Kurten chronicled a life of depravity that began, predictably, with an unhappy, poverty-stricken childhood and an abusive, alcoholic father. At age nine, a neighbor introduced him to the grotesque pleasures of animal torture and bestiality. While still a child, he drowned a friend in the Rhine River. As a teenager, he became a prolific arsonist and raped and slaughtered sheep, goats, and pigs on a regular basis.

After his release from a two-year prison term for theft, he killed his first young girl during a sexual assault. Fortunately, Kurten spent more than 20 of the next 30 years in prison on various robbery and assault charges. Otherwise, his body count probably would have been much higher.

His trial revealed that on May 25, 1913, he killed his first verified victim as the Vampire of Düsseldorf. During the course of a robbery, he came upon 13-year-old Christine Klein asleep in her bed. He slit her throat with a penknife, and he claimed the spurting of her blood excited him. Kurten admitted that he not only relished the act of murder; he also liked to drink the blood of his victims.

But his murderous escapades were over. Kurten was convicted and sentenced to death for the murder of nine women and children and the attempted murder of seven others. It is certain, however, that the number of his victims far exceeded that total. He hinted in his trial that he could not remember the specifics of several others he had killed. Peter Kurten was executed on July 2, 1931, at Klingelputz Prison in Cologne. He seemed to look forward to the event, a beheading. Perhaps the experience of his own death was the only possible climax for his gruesome blood lust.

HENRI LANDRU

THE OUTBREAK OF WORLD WAR I IN 1914 PRESENT-
ED HENRI LANDRU WITH HIS GREATEST OPPORTUNITY
FOR FRAUD AND DECEIT: HE WOULD PREY UPON
VULNERABLE WAR WIDOWS.

Henri Landru was not the picture of a great lover. Yellowing photographs of him show a small, balding man in his fifties wearing a full beard. Yet by his own accounting he had been the lover of 283 women. Ten of these he had married and murdered.

After the fairy-tale character who killed his wives, Henri Landru was called "Bluebeard." The people of his native France didn't condone his killings, but they secretly admired his prowess as a seducer and lover. And yet nothing in the trial records, the testimony of his surviving lovers, or photographs of Landru can explain his success with women. Even his trial jury, who found him guilty within an hour and a half of deliberation, was sufficiently charmed by Landru to recommend leniency.

Henri Landru was born in Paris in 1869. Although his parents were honest and forthright, Henri seems to have preferred the irregular life from the very beginning. Prior to his spree of murder, he had been convicted seven times for fraud. In 1891, he took a second cousin, Mlle. Remy, as his mistress. The young mademoiselle gave birth to a child. Landru then married the girl in 1893, and they subsequently had a second child. Landru drifted from job to job and from scheme to scheme. His wife patiently waited for him through his prison terms; they had four children in all. Landru's retired father, distressed by his son, was apparently less understanding than Landru's wife, and he committed suicide in 1912.

The outbreak of world war in 1914 presented Henri Landru with his greatest opportunity for fraud and deceit: He would prey upon vulnerable war widows. By placing matrimonial ads in newspapers, he collected replies from interested women.

Between 1914 and 1919, Landru sifted through what he claimed were hundreds of applicants to finally marry and murder ten women. They were: Anna Colomb, Celestine Buisson, Jeanne Cruchet (her 18-year-old son disappeared with her), Thérèse Laborde-Line, Madame Heon, Desirée Guillin, Andrée Babelay, Louise Jaume, Anne-Marie Pascal, and Marie-Thérèse Marchadier.

By maintaining two apartments in Paris and a pair of country villas, and by employing a plethora of fake names, Landru was able to juggle several prospective brides and mistresses at once. Once he married a mark, Landru would assume all her accounts and property. He would either sell her furniture or store it at one of his villas. A small outdoor stove on the property of one villa was used by Landru to burn the bodies of his victims.

Like earlier wife killers Johann Hoch and George Joseph Smith, Henri Landru was finally caught by the persistence of his victims' relatives. When the sisters of Anna Colomb and Celestine Buisson lost contact with them, they reported the matter to the police. Unfortunately, the only name the sisters could report was the false one that Landru had been using at the time.

Still, by April 10, 1919, careful police work had determined that the missing women were connected to a single individual who used a variety of aliases. A warrant was issued for that person in the names of the various aliases. By an odd stroke of luck, the sister of Celestine Buisson saw the man she knew as M. Dupont on the streets of Paris with another woman, just two days after reporting her sister's disappearance. She followed the couple into a china shop and observed as they ordered a set of dinnerware. Celestine Buisson's sister, Mlle. Lacoste, reported this find to the Paris police. The police were thus able to track down the couple via an address left at the china shop.

At 76 Rue de Rochechouart, the police encountered Henri Landru with a new mistress, Fernande Segret, to whom he was engaged. When confronted with charges, he denied everything, but he was observed trying to dispose of a small black notebook. It contained meticulous records of all expenses and assets related to his marriage and murder schemes.

The notebook alone was sufficient evidence to convict Landru of all ten murders, and it suggested his involvement in many others. Landru spent two years in jail while French justice untangled the whole sordid story.

Landru's belated trial was front-page news around the world. As the presiding judge laid out the facts in a precise and orderly fashion, Landru sat, bewildered by it all. When asked to clarify points or give testimony, Landru gave deadpan, sarcastic answers that suggested he regarded the whole affair as a trivial joke. His persistent cry throughout the trial was, "Produce your bodies!" He repeatedly insisted that all ten women had merely left him of their own free will and would perhaps show up at the trial to exonerate him. They never did.

Much anticipated was the testimony of Fernande Segret, the sole surviving fiancée. The judge questioned her carefully about Landru's sexual habits, looking perhaps for some evidence of perversity that might have tarnished Landru's Bluebeard aura. But Mlle. Segret would only say that he was a most tender and considerate lover. She revealed that she remained infatuated with the man despite what she now knew about him. In the end, Mlle. Segret's testimony was hardly necessary to convict Landru—the evidence against him was overwhelming.

Henri Landru walked briskly to his execution at the guillotine on February 25, 1922. He was unrepentant and in good humor, saying of the executioner, "I must not keep this gentleman waiting." He didn't.

NATHANIEL LEOPOLD AND RICHARD LOEB

THE TWO YOUNG GENIUSES DECIDED THEY COULD COMMIT THE PERFECT CRIME.

In the 1920s, Nathaniel Leopold, 19, and Richard Loeb, 18, were young men from wealthy families in the fashionable Chicago neighborhood of Hyde Park. Each was intelligent enough to be called a genius and had already graduated from college. Each felt his intelligence made him superior to ordinary people. Their mutual conceit caused them to become friends.

Leopold believed in the "superman" theory of the philosopher Nietzsche and felt they both qualified as supermen. In the spring of 1924, the two young men were casting around for something to interest them, something that would prove their superiority without a doubt. They decided they could commit the perfect crime.

Leopold and Loeb decided to kidnap and murder one of the other young sons of millionaires in Hyde Park. They could collect a healthy ransom and spend the summer traveling in Europe. On the ordained day, May 21, 1924, they waited outside the local prep school in a rented car, planning to select a boy at random. Bobby Franks, Loeb's 14-year-old distant cousin, came by on his way to tennis practice. Bobby knew and looked up to the older boys. When invited, he happily got into the car. He sat in the front seat beside Nathan Leopold, who was driving. After a few blocks, Richard Loeb picked up a heavy chisel in the back seat and jabbed it into the back of Bobby Franks's skull. The boy bled to death in the car within 15 minutes. They drove the body to a marshland on the far south edge of the city where Nathan Leopold often went bird-watching. Then they stripped Bobby naked, poured acid on his face, and stuffed his body into a drainpipe. They drove back to Loeb's home and played cards until midnight. At that point, they phoned in their first ransom notice to Bobby's parents.

Contrary to the geniuses' plans, a workman found the body of Bobby Franks the very next day. This untimely event eliminated the possibility of ransom and was the beginning of their undoing. A thorough police search of the area turned up a pair of spectacles of unique design. The eyeglasses belonged to Nathan Leopold, and the police traced them to him within eight days. Under interrogation, Nathan offered the plausible explanation that he'd lost that pair of glasses on a bird-watching expedition a few days earlier. When the police found some inconsistencies in the youths' testimony, they brought the villainous intellectuals back for a more intensive interrogation on May 31. Richard Loeb was the first to crack under the strain. Both prodigies gave the police a full confession, most of which got leaked to a demanding Chicago press corps. The papers dubbed them the "Thrill Kill Killers" and ran coupons for readers to write in for a chance to be the executioner of Leopold and Loeb.

In this rising tide of public fury at the self-proclaimed supermen, the parents of Leopold and Loeb felt they needed special help to prevent a lynching, even in a large city like Chicago. Prosecutors and policemen were more likely to play politics than dispense justice. The parents hired wily criminal attorney Clarence Darrow, who promised them that he would save their sons from the gallows.

Darrow set about trying to refashion the public's perception of these two super-brats. He tried to cast the two lads as mentally brilliant but emotionally stunted. At the trial, Darrow dwelt on their upbringing: their socialite, millionaire parents who were never around; their isolation; and the development of their warped value systems. Much of this testimony centered on the new science of

Freudian psychology and sexual deviations.

The newspapers and the public ate up Darrow's Freudian strategy—it turned their morning paper into some kind of secret sex manual. Because the young men had pleaded guilty, no jury was present throughout the lengthy trial. Although the judge was not much impressed with Darrow's contention, he realized that it had lowered the public's temper about vigilante justice. He gave each defendant life plus 99 years—they were spared from the death sentence.

In prison, Richard Loeb was knifed to death by a fellow prisoner in 1936. It was reported to be self-defense against Loeb's homosexual advances. Nathan Leopold was a model prisoner. He was paroled in 1958, when luminaries such as Carl Sandburg spoke in his behalf. On his release, Leopold moved to Puerto Rico and lived quietly until his death in 1971.

JOHN LIST

USING HIS FAITH TO JUSTIFY HIS ACTIONS, LIST MURDERED FIVE FAMILY MEMBERS IN HIS OWN HOME. "BY KILLING THEM, THEY WOULD DIE CHRISTIANS," HE TOLD HIS PASTOR.

Forty-six years old, John List had an ideal life. He was a devout Christian and active family man, with a steady job and a loving family. He had taken in his mother to live with him and his family in their 19-room mansion. All seemed perfect.

What happened around November 9, 1971, no one will ever know. The bodies of his family members were found in the family home on December 7, when patrolmen responded to a call from a neighbor. The Westfield, New Jersey, home had been brightly lit for several weeks, which alarmed the neighbor. To their horror, the police found the five decomposed bodies of List's wife, his three children, and his mother. All had been shot to death and neatly arranged in a row. But List was nowhere to be found. He left behind his wallet and driver's license. In 1972, less than one year after the killings, a fire mysteriously destroyed the List mansion.

It seemed that List was $11,000 behind on two mortgages and was facing bank foreclosure on his house. Moreover, his wife Helen was stricken with an incurable and progressively debilitating brain disease, and List believed Helen drank heavily. Worse still, his daughter Patricia was an aspiring actress whom List believed was experimenting with marijuana. The morally rigid List could not tolerate all this. In a letter unearthed later, List confessed to his pastor that "by killing them, they would die Christians."

List eluded capture for 18 years. Renaming himself Robert P. Clark, he moved to Denver, Colorado, and married Delores Miller in 1985. Later they moved near Richmond, Virginia.

In April 1989, the television program *America's Most Wanted* aired a segment that focused on List's deeds. Among the viewers was Wanda Flannery, an acquaintance of Delores Clark from Denver. Wanda recognized List as the man who called himself Bob Clark. She notified the FBI, and Clark was arrested in June 1989. Identified by fingerprints and a scar behind his ear as John List, he was charged with the 1971 murders of his five family members. List is currently awaiting trial.

THE EARL OF LUCAN

IN A VICIOUS CASE OF MISTAKEN IDENTITY, VENGEFUL LORD LUCAN BLUDGEONED TO DEATH HIS CHILDREN'S NANNY.

Richard John Bingham, the seventh Earl of Lucan, wanted custody of his children. After separating from his wife Lady Veronica Lucan, and losing custody of his children, the indebted gambler concocted a wild scheme to get them back, and ended up killing the nanny of his beloved children and brutally injuring his wife.

On November 7, 1974, nanny Sandra Rivett's night out, Lord Lucan sneaked into Lady Lucan's house and hid. He unscrewed the basement light bulb and waited for his wife to descend for her nightly tea in the basement breakfast room. Footsteps announced an approaching woman, whom Lucan viciously clubbed to death. As he doubled the body over and pressed it into a mailbag, he heard a call from the house upstairs: "Sandra . . . Sandra . . . ." Lucan immediately realized that he'd killed the nanny, not his wife. So he waited until Veronica entered the basement. He attacked, and Veronica fought back, tore at his private parts, and escaped.

About 9:45 P.M., Lady Veronica Lucan burst into London's Plumber's Arms pub and hysterically cried, "Help me . . . he murdered the nanny." Police and ambulance were summoned, and Lady Lucan was sped to St. George's Hospital. At the Lucan home, officers searched the basement. They found a canvas mailbag into which a woman's body had been rudely stuffed, folded so the feet were at the head. Detectives discovered a blood-stained, nine-inch lead pipe wrapped in tape. Lord Lucan had vanished.

The fugitive Lucan phoned his mother, imploring her to take the children. He drove to the English Channel, took his speedboat out, and scuttled it, perhaps intending to accompany it to the bottom.

The hospital doctors attended to Lady Lucan's scalp wounds and numerous cuts inside her mouth. On the next morning, she formally accused her husband, Lord Lucan, 39, of murdering Mrs. Rivett and also attempting to murder her.

A coroner's inquest on June 16, 1975, concluded that Sandra Rivett's death was "murder by Lord Lucan." Missing at the time of the inquest, Lucan is still unaccounted for.

HENRY LEE LUCAS

IS HENRY LEE LUCAS THE MOST PROLIFIC SERIAL KILLER IN HISTORY OR MERELY A SKILLFUL LIAR ALTERNATELY HORRIFYING HIS LISTENERS AND PLAYING ON THEIR SYMPATHIES?

To this day, authorities don't know whether to believe Henry Lucas's confessions. At one point, he claimed to have indulged in sufficient violence to turn nearly the whole South into a cemetery of his victims.

What Lucas says of his early years in Blacksburg, Virginia, portrays the perfect breeding ground for a later career of depravity. He claimed that his mother repeatedly beat him senseless with broom handles, deprived him of food for days on end, dressed him in girl's clothes, and forced him to watch her have sex with her many lovers.

Some of these stories are confirmed by neighbors, who also recount that Lucas's father also suffered punishment from the mother. He was an alcoholic who slipped under a moving freight train while he was drunk and lost his legs in the accident. He died of pneumonia in 1950, apparently because he stayed outside in the snow one night to avoid brutal treatment from his wife.

His father's death fueled Lucas's hatred of women to the exploding point. Lucas once maintained that he committed his first murder at 14, killing the first girl with whom he had sex. Before he was finally arrested in Texas in 1983, Lucas supposedly added some 600 more victims to the list, including his mother and his common-law wife, Frieda "Becky" Powell.

While Lucas lived with homosexual Ottis Elwood Toole in Florida, he met Powell, Toole's 12-year-old niece. Becky was taken as Lucas's common-law wife. According to Lucas, during her three years with Lucas, Becky helped him lure victims—men, women, and children—into deadly traps and then watched as he slaughtered them. She also helped Lucas and her Uncle Ottis execute two police officers.

On August 24, 1981, Becky herself fell victim to her lover, paying the price of her life of violence. Lucas says that in a grassy field on the outskirts of Denton, Texas, Becky and Lucas camped for the evening. The couple continued their disagreement about which direction their travels should take them. Becky wanted to return to Florida to visit relatives; Lucas did not. Her temper raged, and she slapped him. He sank a large knife deep into her chest, killing her instantly.

Lucas's lust was aroused, and he raped the life-less body. When the sex act was complete, he sev-ered Becky's head from her body, then her hands, arms, and legs. Lucas scattered the remains around the open field and fled the area. After his arrest, he confessed to hundreds of murders, one of which was Becky's. Remorsefully, Lucas told lawmen he had killed Becky, the only girl he had ever loved.

Lucas has since recanted his boast of 600 mur-ders, stating he is actually guilty of only one—his mother's, in 1960. According to Lucas, he and his mother argued, and she hit him with a broom. The familiar punishment triggered his rage; he hit her once in the throat and then noticed the blood and the knife in his hand. Lucas later said, "I killed my mother for the same reason I've killed all these other women. The reason was sex. I've killed women everywhere. . . . I've never decided ahead of time that I was going to kill a woman. It can happen anytime."

Psychiatrists have theorized that Lucas came alive only in the act of murder. He gained sexual potency after bludgeoning or strangling his sex partner to death. He then had intercourse with the victim's remains.

Lucas became a bisexual after two long prison stints—the second for slaying his mother. He then broadened his homicidal activities to include men as well as women. While in one of his confessional moods, Lucas said that he and Ottis Toole (his killing partner in the months just prior to his arrest) would often commit a murder for no other reason than to have something to do. Thus was Lucas dubbed the "recreational killer." When he had the right audience while in custody in Texas, Lucas would also sometimes confess to acts of cannibalism and bestiality, while Toole offered corroboration via telephone from his prison cell in Jacksonville, Florida.

Lucas was finally apprehended in June 1983 for possessing a gun. Ruben Moore, a preacher at the House of Prayer in Stoneberg, Texas, turned him in to local authorities. Within weeks, after experiencing what he called a religious conversion, Lucas began confessing to scores of murders across the southern half of the United States. The murder that most stirred the public's imagination was that of an unidentified woman in her mid-twenties. Her body—clad only in a pair of orange socks—was found in Texas along Interstate 35. Lucas's graphic confession to the rape/murder of the Jane Doe female induced a San Angelo jury to sentence him to death by lethal injection. But on November 29, 1990, just days before his scheduled execution, Lucas was granted a stay on the basis of the many obvious lies he had told in other confessions. In addition, Toole stated that he had committed the murder himself.

In late 1990, Lucas was extradited to Florida to stand trial for four murders that had occurred between December 15, 1980, and April 9, 1981. Besides the death sentence in Texas, Lucas has also been sentenced to six life prison terms, two 75-year sentences, and a 60-year term for other murder convictions. After initially trying to take credit for virtually every murder in the United States during the past two decades, Lucas now contends he is innocent of everything except the slaying of his mother. In a recent interview he said, "They're just conspiring to get all the unsolved murders pinned on me. I can't see why they're spending all this money on me and letting guilty people run free."

THE McCRARY FAMILY

THE DRIFTERS WERE LINKED TO AS MANY AS 22 MURDERS FROM FLORIDA TO CALIFORNIA.

The vagabond McCrary family drifted through the American Southwest in the early 1970s, leaving a trail of bodies behind them. The FBI sought them in connection with 11 murders in the region. However, at one point, the family was linked to as many as 22 murders between Florida and California. The family consisted of the family patriarch, Sherman McCrary; his wife, Carolyn; their son, Danny; their daughter, Ginger Taylor; and her husband, Raymond Carl Taylor.

The nomadic McCrarys drifted out of Texas and through the Southwest. Their habit was to rob grocery stores in the early evenings. The male McCrarys would rape the women store clerks, who were then shot and killed. The women McCrarys did not object to the rapes or the murders. Instead, they considered it normal manly behavior. In fact, after her capture, Carolyn McCrary said she stayed with her husband because she loved him.

The family's downfall began on June 16, 1972,

when Raymond Taylor robbed a California grocery store and shot a police officer in the process. Witnesses reported his license plate number, and police traced the car to the McCrary residence. Sherman McCrary and Taylor were arrested and charged with two other grocery store robberies. The two pleaded guilty to both counts and received five-year prison terms. Carolyn, Danny, and Ginger received nine-month sentences for harboring felons.

However, as detectives investigated the case, they linked the family to more than 20 murders throughout the region. Sherman McCrary, a 47-year-old alcoholic, had spent time in jail for robbery; son-in-law Taylor had too. McCrary said he took to armed robbery because he had a bad back and could never find a decent job.

The family's first known victim was Sheri Martin, kidnapped from a Salt Lake City bakery in August of 1971. She was raped and then shot with a .32-caliber weapon. The family stole $200 from the register. A month later, her body was found, naked from the waist down, near Wendover, Nevada. About a week later, the family abducted Leeora Looney from a shop in suburban Denver. She was raped and shot with the same .32-caliber weapon used on Martin. Looney's naked body was found 200 miles away three days after the abduction. A string of abductions followed. Elizabeth

Perryman disappeared from a Lubbock, Texas, restaurant in September. In October, Forrest and Jena Covey vanished from the Mesquite, Texas, grocery store they owned. Three days later, 16-year-old Susan Shaw was abducted from a cake shop only a few blocks away. Police pulled Shaw's body from nearby Lake Ray Hubbard shortly after her kidnapping. They also found the Coveys' bodies that day in a Quinlan, Texas, barn. They had been bound and shot with a .32-caliber gun. Perryman's skeleton was found by an area farmer in December.

In November, the bloody trail led to Florida, where the bodies of two women hairdressers were found shot and naked in the back of their shop. The 16-year-old daughter of one of the hairdressers had been abducted. Her decomposed body was found in a wooded area near Jacksonville, Florida. A lack of clothing suggested she had been raped.

In November of 1972, Sherman McCrary, Carolyn McCrary, and Taylor were indicted for the abduction and murder of Looney. Danny McCrary was indicted in December. Charges soon followed in connection with Martin's death. Ginger McCrary was eventually indicted for passing a phony check in Denver. By the time it was over, police were able to directly connect the family to 11 other brutal murders.

CAPTAIN JEFFREY MacDONALD

THE GREEN BERET CAPTAIN RAVED THAT A BAND OF DRUG-CRAZED HIPPIES HAD INVADED THE HOME, CHANTING "ACID IS GROOVY, KILL THE PIGS!"

When military police at Fort Bragg, North Carolina, came to the apartment of Captain Jeffrey MacDonald on the morning of February 17, 1970, they found the bloody bodies of the captain's family. His pregnant wife, 26-year-old Colette, lay dead in one of the bedrooms. The word "pig" was scrawled in blood on the headboard of the bed. Their two daughters, five-year-old Kimberly and two-year-old Kristen, lay in two other bedrooms. Captain MacDonald, 26, was on the floor beside his wife, but his wounds were later revealed to be only minor. He raved to the medics who attended him that a band of drug-crazed hippies had invaded the home, chanting "Acid is groovy, kill the pigs!"

Captain MacDonald said he was asleep on the living room couch when he was awakened by screaming. He fought with the intruders, who clubbed him and stabbed him in the chest.

MacDonald described the frenzied attackers as three men accompanied by a woman with long, blonde hair who was wearing a floppy hat and carrying a candle.

Army investigators were skeptical of MacDonald's story. Six weeks later, with no break in the bizarre case, the Army announced that MacDonald himself, a Princeton-educated doctor from New York, was a suspect. However, a closed-door hearing recommended that no charges be pursued against the captain. MacDonald applied for and received an honorable discharge.

In 1971, the Army's Criminal Investigation Department (CID) reopened the investigation. The FBI made extensive laboratory tests of bloodstains and other physical evidence. The agents again interrogated MacDonald. An informant offered a tip that a young woman in the hippie district of Fayetteville, North Carolina, matched MacDonald's description of the blonde. The woman and several of her men friends, all drug users, were questioned and discounted as suspects.

A June 1971 CID report to the Justice Department concluded that all evidence still pointed to the Green Beret doctor. The case remained at a stalemate until 1974, when the known facts were presented to a federal grand jury at Raleigh, North Carolina.

The grand jury heard 75 witnesses including

MacDonald. On January 24, 1975, the grand jury indicted the doctor on three counts of murder. His trial took place in federal court in Raleigh. Federal prosecutors presented a strong circumstantial case based largely on the bloodstain evidence, which showed inconsistencies in MacDonald's story of what had happened. In August 1975, the jury found him guilty of second-degree murder in the deaths of Colette and Kimberly and first-degree murder in Kristen's killing, which the jury decided was calculated to cover up the other murders. Jeffrey MacDonald received three consecutive life sentences.

Acting on grounds that the long delay between the crime and the trial had denied the doctor's rights to a speedy trial, the U.S. Fourth Circuit Court of Appeals in July 1980 set aside the trial verdict and ordered dismissal of the indictment. MacDonald was freed on bail, and he returned to California to resume his pretrial lifestyle in a luxury condo, mixing with wealthy friends. However, his bubble burst in March 1983, when the U.S. Supreme Court reversed the appellate court action and ordered MacDonald back to prison to serve the sentences imposed at his trial. Two months earlier, the blonde hippie drug addict who had been a suspect died of natural causes.

Nevertheless, the hippie gang theory continued to haunt the case. In October 1990, MacDonald's attorneys filed a motion for a new trial, claiming that evidence in the FBI's possession had not been disclosed at the time of the trial. The motion alleged that the withheld evidence—black wool fibers and a blonde wig strand found at the death scene—would verify MacDonald's story that outsiders had murdered his family on that terrible day 20 years ago. The motion is still pending at this writing.

CHARLES MANSON

MANSON BELIEVED A RACE WAR WAS IMMINENT IN WHICH THE BLACKS WOULD CONQUER THE WHITES. HIS PLAN WAS TO ACCELERATE THIS WAR BY MURDERING WHITES IN SUCH A WAY THE "PIGS" WOULD BLAME THE BLACKS.

Charles Manson's mother was Kathleen Maddox, who was 16 years old at the time of his birth. She lived with a succession of men and eventually married William Manson. A promiscuous woman, she spent little time disciplining Charles and allowed him to do whatever he wanted. Charles alternated his time between this permissive atmosphere and the repressive atmosphere of an aunt who was very strict.

When he was 12, his school characterized him as being moody and having a persecution complex. He committed a number of burglaries, including car thefts, and was sent to juvenile centers. He repeatedly ran away from them. At age 13, Manson had already committed his first armed robbery. He soon became involved with more serious crimes. When he was 17, his aunt offered to take him in, and he had a chance to start leading a normal life in a stable environment. Manson was due for a parole hearing. But he became involved in violence again. He held a razor blade to another boy's throat and sodomized him. Manson was sent to a federal reformatory.

Manson went through a change. His work habits and education improved, and in 1954, at the age of 19, he was granted parole to stay with his aunt and uncle. He joined his mother for a while, but in 1955 he married a 17-year-old girl. Although Manson took various jobs, he also stole cars, taking two or more across state lines. He drove one from Ohio to California where, accompanied by his pregnant wife, he was arrested. They ultimately got divorced.

In and out of jails for escalating offenses from robbery to procuring (prostitutes) to forgery, Manson had spent half his life in prison when he was finally released from jail in the late 1960s into a world of upheaval. Those were the days of LSD and heroin, of Flower Power and Stop the War, and of long-haired kids and nonstop sex. It was heaven to Manson.

By the age of 34, Manson had gathered together a group of drifters and hippies. Some of his "family" were misfits—young, middle-class girls who felt unwanted and craved love, freedom, and admiration. His family also included some ex-cons, bums, punks, and musicians. Manson made them feel important—part of an exciting mission.

These cultists worshipped Manson, viewing him as a mix of Jesus Christ and the devil. Often he played his guitar and sang. Under the guise of pseudoreligious rites, Manson led his group in free love, drug experimentation, and sexual perversions. As time went on, his followers also practiced guerrilla tactics.

After moving around awhile, he set up a commune at an old Hollywood filming location—the Spahn Ranch near Los Angeles. Various Hollywood personalities supplied money in the beginning so the Manson family could buy food and other necessities. At times, they raided garbage cans. One of the girls, Lynette "Squeaky" Fromme, was assigned to keep the elderly, half-blind owner of the ranch, George Spahn, happy.

Manson, who has a high IQ, believed a race war was imminent in which the blacks would conquer the whites. He called this war "Helter Skelter," and he preached of it often to his followers, noting that it was also the title of a Beatles song. Manson's plan was to accelerate this war by murdering whites in such a way that the "pigs" (the establishment) would blame the blacks. Before the war's culmination, Manson and his family—comprising at its peak more than 40 members—would escape to the hills.

In the summer of 1969, Manson started talking murder. Soon after, he shot a black drug dealer who had allegedly crossed him. The man recovered and didn't press charges.

Shortly thereafter, Manson sent cult members Bobby Beausoleil, Susan Atkins, and Mary Brunner to Gary Hinman's house. The supposed purpose of their visit was to invite Hinman to join their family, but in reality it was to rob him of the $20,000 rumored to be in his possession. When Beausoleil called his leader to say he couldn't find the cash, Manson drove over and nearly cut off Hinman's ear with a sword. The gang made Hinman sign over possession of his cars before stabbing him, at Manson's orders, and leaving him to die. Beausoleil wrote "Political Piggy" in blood on the wall. He also drew a panther paw to make the police think the radical Black Panthers had committed the murder.

One week after Hinman was found, the police stopped Beausoleil, and seeing the transfer document to Hinman's car, they held him. The police also arrested family members Sandra Good and Mary Brunner for using stolen credit cards. Upset, Manson claimed it was time for Helter Skelter on August 9, 1969.

Charles "Tex" Watson, Patricia Krenwinkel,

Susan Atkins, and Linda Kasabian—all part of the Manson family and high on hallucinogens—went to Cielo Drive in the hills above Hollywood. At the secluded home of film producer Roman Polanski, who was abroad, they murdered his pregnant wife Sharon Tate. In addition, they killed four others— Abigail Folger, coffee heiress; her lover, Voityck Frykowski, Polish writer and producer; Jay Sebring, noted hair stylist; and Steven Parent, who had been visiting the mansion's caretaker. As he unloaded his pistol into the hapless victims, Watson kept screaming, "I am the devil, and I've come to do the devil's work!" During the slaughter, the victims were stabbed, hanged, shot, and clubbed. Their blood was used to write such slogans as "Pig" and "War" on the walls. The atrocities, according to Susan Atkins later, were copycat versions of Hinman's murder. Linda Kasabian, lookout for the killers, lost her nerve during the merciless massacre and later turned witness for the prosecution.

The murders caused panic in Hollywood. Manson was pleased. Within hours, he led the next slaughter himself. The Tate killers accompanied him; so did Clem Grogan and Leslie van Houten. As before, they were all high on drugs. The hideous scene of Cielo Drive was repeated at the home of Leno and Rosemary LaBianca. A fork was left in Leno's flesh and "War" was carved on his

---

abdomen; "Helter Skelter" (misspelled), "Death to Pigs," and "Rise" were written in blood on the refrigerator and walls. After the murder, the group took showers, ate, and fed the victims' dogs.

Although Manson and 20 family members were arrested a few days later when the police raided the Spahn Ranch, it was for suspicion of car theft. No proof was found, and they were released.

In October, Bobby Beausoleil's girlfriend, who had quit the family once but returned, was taken to jail for the Hinman murder. She denied involvement but named the two women who were there—Susan Atkins and Mary Brunner. Although Atkins also denied the Hinman charge, she boasted to a cellmate, Virginia Graham, that she'd taken part in the Tate-LaBianca murders. At first, the woman thought she was crazy, hearing Atkins rave on about Charlie being "love, pure love" and how "it feels good when the knife goes in." But Graham told her friend Ronnie Howard, who occupied the same cell, about it. Hearing more, Graham realized the girl was telling the truth, but when she tried to tell lawmen, she was ignored. It was Howard, a former call girl, who finally reached someone who would listen, and the murder story reached the Los Angeles police chief.

As a result, Watson, Krenwinkel, Kasabian, and later Manson, Atkins, and van Houten were charged with the Tate-LaBianca slayings.

Throughout the much-publicized trial, the women maintained Manson's innocence, shaving their heads in protest of his confinement. Not one showed remorse. Before long, all members of Manson's family involved in these murders, the Hinman slaying, and the killing of Donald "Shorty" Shea—a bit-part cowboy actor whose body was never found—were found guilty except for Linda Kasabian and Mary Brunner. In a separate trial, Bobby Beausoleil was given life imprisonment, as was Susan Atkins. Charles Manson and the others were sentenced to death. However, because the California Supreme Court abolished the death penalty in 1972, their sentences were altered to life imprisonment.

Manson boasted of having committed 35 murders. Although the exact number has never been established, Vincent Bugliosi, the prosecuting attorney, believed the number may have even exceeded Manson's estimate.

HERMANN WEBSTER MUDGETT
"H. H. HOLMES"

A SMALL-TIME SWINDLER BECAME AMERICA'S FIRST SERIAL KILLER.

Hermann Webster Mudgett was a nineteenth-century swindler who also has the distinction of being considered America's first serial killer. A seducer, bigamist, and murderer, he was involved with a host of women and a variety of confidence scams. When police finally searched his mansion on 63rd Street in Chicago's Englewood area, they removed the remains of many of his victims, including human skulls, teeth, and bones. Police found a blood-stained dissecting table in the basement and charred bones in a nearby stove.

The house itself was a labyrinth, containing winding passages and hidden rooms with peepholes and trapdoors. A complex network of pipes had been installed to pump gas into some rooms. Mudgett reportedly had the three-story house built in shifts, firing work crews every few weeks so no one would learn the mansion's secrets. Eventually, the home was dubbed his "murder castle."

Born in New Hampshire in 1860, Mudgett reportedly became fascinated with cadavers when his schoolmates, playing a prank, dragged him into a surgery room where there was a skeleton. While studying medicine at 18, he orchestrated his first scam—an insurance fraud in which he faked a patient's death. Eight years after he married, he abandoned his wife and child and moved to Chicago. Adopting the name H. H. Holmes, he bigamously married a well-to-do socialite. He had a falling out with her family after he forged her uncle's signature on a document.

Soon, Holmes began his career of erratic murders. He killed his first victim, a friend named Dr. Robert Leacock, for life insurance. Holmes then became the assistant and, later, partner of a drug store on 63rd Street in Englewood. However, after rumors of rigged books and threats of prosecution, the owner mysteriously disappeared, and H. H. Holmes took over sole ownership.

Business thrived in the early 1890s, and he began construction of a mansion that he planned to use as a hotel for the 1893 Chicago World's Fair. Holmes's second wife remained with her family in Wilmette, a Chicago suburb. Soon, Julia Conner and her husband, a jeweler, moved into the mansion. The husband worked in a shop on the ground floor. However, he left his wife after he realized she and Holmes were lovers. Conner became pregnant and died during a botched abortion attempt. Holmes later poisoned the woman's daughter so that she would not speak about her mother's death.

Several murders followed in sequence. First, a fishing companion was killed for the cash he was carrying. Next, a business speculator was also eliminated for money. Finally, Holmes murdered a female domestic servant to keep his janitor from running away with her. He eventually took another mistress, Emily Cigrand. When she told him she was getting married, he became so jealous that he lured her into one of the rooms, locked her in, and turned on the gas. He watched her die a painfully slow death.

Eventually, he met a man named Benjamin Pitezel, who became his partner. He also took another mistress, Minnie Williams, who became an accomplice in his con games. Holmes fled Chicago after a failed insurance scam in which he set fire to his mansion. By that time, he had murdered Minnie, too.

In St. Louis, he met Georgiana Yoke and married her. A mortgage fraud landed Holmes in jail, where he met the famous train robber Marion Hedgepeth. The two worked out an insurance-murder swindle that eventually led to Holmes's demise. In that swindle, Holmes staged Pitezel's accidental death and collected on his insurance policy. However, he didn't square up with Hedgepeth, and the insurance company realized it had been defrauded. Holmes had already killed three of Pitezel's children by the time he was arrested.

Holmes was sentenced to death; he published confessions to 27 murders. Most of the information proved accurate after further investigation of his Chicago home.

Some researchers consider his case more sensational than that of Jack the Ripper. What made him remarkable, they say, is that he was not a born sadist. Holmes/Mudgett was a petty swindler who became a mass murderer by small degrees.

JUDITH ANN AND ALVIN NEELLEY

A MODERN-DAY BONNIE AND CLYDE WENT ON A MURDER SPREE IN THE SOUTH UNTIL THEY GOT CAUGHT FOR WRITING BAD CHECKS.

Judith Neelley's part in several grisly killings in Alabama, Tennessee, and Georgia in the early 1980s earned her the distinction of being the youngest woman on death row. She was 18.

After months of working odd jobs together, passing phony checks, and implementing petty con games, Judith, then age 16, married Alvin Neelley, 27, in Ringgold, Georgia.

The Neelleys both served time shortly after their marriage, because Judith robbed a woman at gunpoint in Rome, Georgia. Alvin served his sentence in the Walker Correctional Institute in Lafayette. Judith, a minor and pregnant, was turned over to the Rome Youth Development Center, where she gave birth to twins two days after her arrival.

While the two were separated, they wrote letters frequently. Judith was released in March of 1981. She was later linked to the fire-bombing of a house that belonged to one of the youth center's staff members, shots fired at another employee's house, and threatening telephone calls made to both houses by a female caller.

Judith lived with her twins and Alvin's parents in Tennessee until her husband was released in April of 1982. Alvin took a job in a gas station. He managed to raise enough money to buy two cars equipped with CB radios. His CB "handle" was "The Nightrider," and she was "Lady Sundance." The two also referred to themselves jokingly as "Boney and Claude," a play on the names of Depression-era outlaws Bonnie and Clyde.

When the robbery and con games became dull, the couple turned to murder. Their first victim was 13-year-old Lisa Ann Millican. The girl, a resident of a home for neglected children, was visiting a shopping mall in Rome, Georgia, when she was abducted. The couple held her captive for several days; she was raped repeatedly by Alvin in hotel rooms. Even more disturbing was Judith's account of injecting shots of drain cleaner into the girl. In his book *Early Graves*, author Thomas Cook recounts an interrogation during which Judith coldly admits to injecting six doses of the lethal liquid into Millican's neck, arms, and buttocks. Judith watched her suffer for half an hour. In spite of the injections, Millican lived on. Eventually, the couple finished the girl off by shooting her. They dumped her body in Alabama's Little River Canyon. Judith made several anonymous telephone calls to local police to report the murder.

The couple then abducted 26-year-old John Hancock and his fiancée, 23-year-old Janice Chatman. Hancock, who survived the ordeal, said Judith shot him in the back. Hancock did not know the Neelleys previously. However, he listened to a tape of the anonymous female caller who reported the Millican death and recognized it as the voice of Judith.

The Neelleys eventually were arrested for writing bad checks in Tennessee. Judith was revealed as the woman who had made threats against the Youth Development Center. Hancock later identified the Neelleys as the couple who had abducted and shot him. Chatman's sexually abused body was found later. She had been shot to death.

In custody, Alvin and Judith turned on each other. Alvin claimed Judith was the impetus behind the murders. Judith said Alvin had threatened to harm her children if she did not capture women for him to rape. Police estimated the couple had murdered as many as 15 people.

Alvin received two life sentences after pleading guilty to murder. Jurors recommended life in prison for Judith's role in the Millican death. A judge ignored the recommendation and sentenced her to death row.

EARLE LEONARD NELSON

POSING AS A BIBLE SALESMAN, HE WOULD TAKE LODGINGS IN A BOARDING HOUSE. IN SHORT ORDER, HE WOULD RAPE AND STRANGLE THE LANDLADY.

Born in Philadelphia, Pennsylvania, in 1897, Earle Leonard Nelson was orphaned at an early age. His Aunt Lillian, an obsessively religious woman, raised him in a strict environment that heavily relied on the Bible for guidance. After all, it was her intention that young Earle become a minister when he grew up.

Obedient to a fault, Earle was a model child with impeccable manners who read the Bible daily. Although his behavior pleased his Aunt Lillian greatly, he was the type of child that other children love to hate.

Young Earle was in a near-fatal streetcar accident in which his skull was cracked and he almost died. Afterward, he experienced a drastic change in personality. The "perfect gentleman" began to have strange obsessions. Caught peeping at a cousin as she undressed, he became a source of concern to his prudish Aunt Lillian, who was forced to reprimand him for "unclean habits."

In 1917, at the age of 21, Nelson was arrested for attempting to rape the daughter of a next-door neighbor. While serving two years in jail, he attempted to escape several times. Although prison authorities knew that the book had not been closed on Earle Nelson, he was released in late 1919 in accordance with his sentencing.

In an apparent turnabout, Earle changed his name to Roger Wilson, met and married a schoolteacher, and seemed to settle down completely. Nothing was heard from (or known about) him for seven years. While his marriage didn't last very long (the wife blamed Earle's "intense sexual jealousy"), there were no psychotic incidents.

Then, in early 1926, Earle Leonard Nelson just exploded. From one end of the country to the other, he began raping and strangling women. He was called "the Gorilla Murderer" because of his large, throttling hands and the savage fury he possessed as he squeezed the life out of his victims.

Nelson's method and choice of victims remained consistent. Posing as a Bible salesman, he would take lodgings in a boarding house. In short order, he would rape and strangle the landlady. Between February 1926 and June 1927, he murdered 22 women across the United States and Canada.

On June 1, 1927, Nelson raped and killed two sisters; he abducted a blind flower girl on June 3, killing her five days later. He murdered another woman the very next day. This spurt of violent activity called forth a continent-wide manhunt that put real pressure on Nelson, who did not kill again. In November 1927, he was spotted in the village of Wakopa, Canada. An entire army of police, Mounties, and regular army encircled and captured him.

Nelson was taken to Winnipeg, Canada, for trial. The savage killer remained mute and impassive throughout the proceedings. He displayed none of the violence that had typified his rampage, and many questions about the crimes and his motivations went unanswered. While standing on the gallows following his conviction, however, Nelson broke his silence and asked for forgiveness from his many victims and from God for his damned soul. The Gorilla Murderer was hanged on January 13, 1928.

BENNIE NG, WILLIE MAK, AND TONY NG

THE THREE ROBBERS THOUGHT THEY HAD LEFT NO SURVIVORS, BUT ONE ELDERLY MAN WAS STILL ALIVE.

The Wah Mee Club in Seattle's Chinatown was a private gambling club known for its high stakes. Benjamin "Bennie" K. Ng, Kwan Fai "Willie" Mak, and Wai-Chiu "Tony" Ng (the Ngs were not related) were three Hong Kong immigrants all in their twenties. They decided to rob the club and leave no witnesses. On February 19, 1983, at 12:30 A.M., the three of them entered the club to do just that.

They bound the hands of the 14 patrons and employees they found in the club. Then they methodically fired bullets into each victim's head at close range. Then they quickly rounded up all the money they could find—about $10,000, considerably less than the $50,000 to $100,000 they expected to find. The three left with the money.

Unknown to the killers, one elderly man was

still alive. The lone survivor managed to free his hands and crawl out the front door. He was soon found by a passerby who notified the police. When the surviving victim's condition had stabilized and he was able to speak, he positively identified Benjamin Ng and Kwan Mak as two of the gunmen. Wai-Chiu Ng was later identified by other police sources as the third gunman.

During the search of the apartment belonging to Benjamin Ng's girlfriend, detectives discovered a considerable sum of money on her bedroom dresser. Ng told them that he had earned it as a dealer at the Hop Sing Club. However, when police found a shoebox containing more than $10,000 in cash, Ng had no explanation. Likewise, he could not explain the presence of two handguns, ammunition, and a rifle found in the apartment.

The lone survivor of "Seattle's Chinatown Massacre" testified, and Benjamin Ng and Kwan Fai Mak were each convicted of 13 counts of murder. Kwan Mak, portrayed as the mastermind, was sentenced to death. Benjamin Ng was sentenced to life imprisonment with no chance of parole. Wai-Chiu Ng was convicted of 13 counts of robbery and sentenced to seven consecutive life terms.

THE NIGHT STALKER
RICHARD RAMIREZ

FULLY ONE YEAR AFTER HIS FIRST KILLING, LOS ANGELES POLICE FINALLY WARNED RESIDENTS TO BEWARE OF THE NIGHT STALKER.

In 1984 and 1985, Southern California was the scene of a series of murders that seemed to have no relation to each other. Not until August 8, 1985, did police link one man to the brutal crimes. Fully one year after his first killing, Los Angeles police finally warned citizens to beware of the Night Stalker. By that time, the Night Stalker—25-year-old Richard Ramirez—had been credited with at least 14 murders, several rapes, and two instances of child molestation.

It was months earlier, on March 17, 1985, that police got their first description of the killer. He murdered Dayle Okazaki, but roommate Maria Hernandez survived and provided the police with a description of a long-faced man with curly hair, bulging eyes, and rotting teeth.

During the months to follow, detectives uncovered an array of murders and assaults in which victims were raped and bludgeoned to death. In some cases, Satanic pentagrams had been inked on their bodies.

At first, the murders were spaced out. Reports came of three killings in a week—and then nothing for more than a month. But by late July, the killings were occurring almost weekly. On some days, the killer would strike twice in different suburbs.

However, police found less to connect the murders than in most cases of serial killings. Some victims had been shot, but two different guns had been used. Others had had their throats cut or were beaten to death. The victims ranged in age from 16 to 84 and included both men and women. Ramirez's oldest victim was 84-year-old Mabel Bell, who was savagely beaten along with her elderly sister. In several attacks, Ramirez had first killed the husband and then raped the wife before beating her to death. When police found the bodies of one married couple who had been fatally stabbed and beaten, they learned the eyes of the wife had been carved out and taken from the house. Other cases involved burglaries—in one report $30,000 worth of cash and jewelry had been stolen. The one common thread was that the killer attacked at night, entering homes through unlocked doors and windows.

Reports were made of Ramirez sexually assaulting and then freeing his victim. In the early stages of his spree, Ramirez seemed more interested in child molestation than murder. One of his early victims was a six-year-old Montebello girl picked up at a bus stop near her school on February 15, 1985. She was carried away in a laundry bag, sexually abused, and dumped off (alive) in Silver Lake. He than kidnapped a nine-year-old girl from her bedroom in Monterey Park, raped her, and left her in Elysian Park.

It is believed that the first time police found Ramirez's fingerprints at a murder scene was in June 1984, when they found a 79-year-old woman dead in her Glassell Park home. But police didn't announce their manhunt for a single suspect, linked to at least six recent murders, until August 8, 1985, after they had discovered three murders within three days.

Ramirez quickly moved the scene of the crime to San Francisco, where he shot a 66-year-old man in his home on August 17, 1985. The man's wife, however, survived a brutal attack to identify a sketch of Ramirez. Though police still did not know the identity of the killer, that would soon end.

On August 22, 1985, Ramirez attacked 29-year-old Bill Carns in his Mission Viejo home. Carns died of a gunshot wound to the head, but his fiancée survived a rape and told police Ramirez fled in a stolen station wagon. Police found the car six days later and, with the help of a new laser detection system, were able to pull a clean set of fingerprints. Ramirez, who had a history of drug abuse and a criminal record including drug and gambling offenses, soon had his picture painted on every television screen and newspaper in southern California.

Police didn't even have to track him down. He was spotted in East Los Angeles attempting to steal a car. When Ramirez tried to pull a woman from her car, he was attacked by the woman's husband with a steel pole. Bystanders recognized him as the Night Stalker, and ultimately police had to rescue Ramirez from the angry mob.

Ramirez was described as a drifter from Texas, rarely employed, heavily into drugs by the age of 12, and always interested in the occult.

By the time he finally was caught, Ramirez had been credited with at least 16 murders (although he was convicted of only 13) and 50 other felonies—including rape, sodomy, oral copulation, burglary, and attempted murder—for which he was found guilty on September 20, 1989. The California jury found 18 separate instances to make Ramirez eligible for the death penalty.

DENNIS ANDREW NILSEN

HE TOLD TALES OF STRANGLING HIS VICTIMS, HACKING THEM UP, AND BOILING THE PIECES.

He was a good cook, his mother said. Indeed, Dennis "Des" Andrew Nilsen had served as a cook in the British royal guard. But what often boiled on his stove was anything but appetizing.

On February 8, 1983, a plumber, attempting to unclog a foul-smelling sewer near Nilsen's London home, found two decomposed heads and other body parts inside the cistern. The plumber alerted his supervisor, who in turn contacted Scotland Yard.

When Nilsen returned from work the following day, a detective met the 37-year-old government employment service worker in the hallway of his apartment building in the Muswell Hill district of north London. The detective wished to question Nilsen about the contents of the sewer.

Nilsen was more than willing to oblige the policeman. He unlocked his door, and the two entered the room. The room reeked. The source of the odor, Nilsen volunteered without emotion, was the decaying flesh of some of his victims. Upon his arrest, Nilsen calmly told the detective that he had killed more than a dozen men, most of whom were homosexual.

Scotland Yard would later discover that Nilsen had mutiltated 15 men, a total surpassing that of the legendary "Yorkshire Ripper," Peter Sutcliffe, who slew 11 women between 1975 and 1980.

Nilsen's grisly tale begins in late December, 1978, when he went to a nearby tavern and enjoyed the company of a young Irishman. They drank heartily, and as the evening wore on, Nilsen invited the young man back to his apartment for a nightcap. It turned out to be the man's last drink.

After the Irishman passed out, Nilsen strangled him with a necktie. He then undressed the corpse and methodically washed it, a ritual he followed with each of his subsequent victims.

Although he burned the young Irishman, Nilsen normally disposed of his victims by dismembering them, boiling the parts, and burying them in a nearby yard.

Nilsen's second attempt at murder failed. At a Salisbury pub, Nilsen picked up a gay Chinese man with a penchant for kinky sex. The man wanted to be tied up on Nilsen's bed. Nilsen obliged and tried to strangle the man.

The man was able to break free. He fled the

apartment and alerted the police. During the ensuing investigation, Nilsen told police that the Chinese man was trying to "rip him off." The investigators bought Nilsen's story. He was free to continue the killing.

A Canadian was Nilsen's second victim. Victim three was a 19-year-old butcher. Both were men Nilsen had met at pubs. And both were strangled to death.

Nilsen's fourth victim was of Latin or Oriental descent. Another Irishman was his fifth victim. Their bodies, like those of his previous two victims, were bathed and boiled.

The string of deaths would continue until February 1, 1983, eight days before his arrest and a week before the plumber would unearth the horrors in the sewer.

Nilsen's trial opened on October 24, 1983. Though he had confessed to 15 slayings, he was charged with only six murders and two attemped murders. Just a few days later, November 24, 1983, the man whose colleague described as "an efficient worker with nothing very remarkable about him" was found guilty on all charges. He received a life sentence.

CARL PANZRAM

HE WAS EVIL IN EVERY SENSE OF THE WORD, AND HE WAS PROUD OF IT.

Each killer has special reasons and circumstances for committing the most vile crime of all. But few killers act with the passionate hatred and lack of remorse that Carl Panzram showed. He was evil in every sense of the word, and he was proud of it. It seems almost impossible that one man could commit as many crimes as he did. Too many have been proved, however, to leave any doubt of Panzram's guilt. "In my lifetime," he stated, "I have murdered 21 human beings, I have committed thousands of burglaries, robberies, larcenies, arsons and last but not least I have committed sodomy on more than 1,000 male human beings. For all these things I am not in the least bit sorry. . . ."

The son of Prussian immigrants, Carl Panzram was born in Warren, Minnesota, in 1891. His life of improper behavior started early. He was arrested for drinking and disorderly conduct when he was only eight years old. At the tender age of 11, Carl went on a robbery rampage and ended up in reform school. The school was never the same after Carl arrived—he burned down the building, causing more than $100,000 in damages. This act of violence pleased him so much that he repeated it. In July of 1905, he burned down a warehouse in St. Paul, Minnesota, for fun. He was sent back to reform school for another year. After his discharge, Carl Panzram took up his life of crime once again and did not stop until he was caught.

Reform school had turned a potential criminal into a confirmed one. Institutional life seemed only to accentuate the monstrous side of his nature. Panzram joined the Army while drunk and spent the next 37 months in military prison rather than be broken by regimental discipline. After his dishonorable discharge, Panzram traveled the world—leaving a trail of raped, murdered bodies behind him.

After a large heist, he rented a yacht and lured several sailors aboard with the promise of free liquor. He drugged them all and raped each in turn. Then he slit their throats, threw them overboard, and sailed away. He called it "a party." In Portuguese West Africa, he hired eight native carriers to help him hunt crocodiles. Instead, he killed them and committed sodomy on their corpses. When he was done, he fed the bodies to the crocodiles.

In 1928, Panzram was arrested for a series of burglaries in the Washington, D.C./Baltimore area. (He was suspected of several murders, but he was not tried for them.) He was convicted of burglary and sentenced to 20 years in federal prison.

On his arrival at Leavenworth, Panzram informed everyone he saw that he would kill the first man who got in his way. True to his word, he crushed the skull of a civilian laundry superintendent named Robert Warnke. That little stunt put Panzram on death row, where, one suspects, he wanted to be. When opponents of capital punishment petitioned for a commutation of his death sentence, he sent them venomous letters. One note threatened, "I wish you all had one neck, and I had my hands on it."

Carl Panzram's final burst of fury was directed at the hangman. As he stood on the platform on September 5, 1930, he berated the executioner for his slowness, and urged him to hurry it up: "I could hang a dozen men while you're fooling around!" Given the chance, he might have.

JOHN PAUL PHILLIPS

WHILE SERVING HIS TIME, PHILLIPS BRAGGED TO A CELL MATE ABOUT THE MURDERS OF CLARK AND McSHARRY.

A pretty 21-year-old woman—a college student at Southern Illinois University in Carbondale, Illinois—was found dead in her apartment on the east side of town on January 27, 1975. The body of Teresa Clark was discovered in a bathtub of water. Her body was covered with multiple stab wounds. Investigation showed she may have been sexually assaulted.

The prime suspect during the investigation was John Paul Phillips, who lived in the same apartment complex. But no physical evidence was found at the scene of the crime to implicate Phillips in the murder.

A second coed was murdered within 18 months of Clark's death. Kathleen McSharry, a 22-year-old student, was found murdered in her apartment at the north end of town. Like Clark, she had died from multiple stab wounds. Investigation of the crime scene revealed that she had fought her assailant. The window of the back door was broken, and furniture had been broken in the bedroom where her body lay, indicating a struggle. Investigators discovered a bloody sheet in the water-filled bathtub. She too was a victim of a sexual assault. Again, Phillips was considered a suspect, but again, no physical evidence pointed to the identity of the killer.

In a small town southeast of Carbondale, Phillips approached a young couple and severely beat the man and handcuffed him to a tree. Phillips kidnapped and raped the woman. Phillips went to prison for this crime. After his release, he returned to his hometown of Carbondale.

On November 11, 1981, the nude body of Joan Weatherall was discovered floating in water in a shallow pit 12 miles from Carbondale. She had been beaten, strangled, and sexually assaulted. The 30-year-old cocktail hostess had been abducted from a Carbondale street. That same year, another Southern Illinois University coed was murdered on the grounds of the campus. She died of strangulation and had been sexually assaulted. Phillips was working at a nearby construction site.

Later that year, Phillips's luck finally ran out. He was arrested in Carterville, Illinois, while trying to abduct a young girl off the street. He was convicted and sentenced to prison. While serving his time, Phillips bragged to a cell mate about the murders of Clark and McSharry. Phillips also confided to the inmate about the murder of Weatherall. Phillips gave details about the murders that only the killer would know. These statements brought murder charges against him in the Weatherall case.

The inmate testified against Phillips during the trial. During that testimony, Phillips—shackled and handcuffed—attempted to shoot the witness with a makeshift weapon of hardened clay around a shotgun shell. As Phillips attempted to strike the primer cap with a nail, he was wrestled to the ground by sheriff's deputies and disarmed.

Phillips was found guilty of the murder of Joan Weatherall and sentenced to death. He now awaits his fate on death row.

ST. VALENTINE'S DAY MASSACRE

A THOROUGHLY SHAKEN BUGS MORAN HAD ONLY ONE COMMENT FOR THE POLICE AND THE PRESS: "ONLY CAPONE KILLS LIKE THAT!"

Throughout the 1920s, Chicago's two great crime syndicates had waged a turf war over bootleg liquor sales. Al Capone and his gang controlled the South Side, and George "Bugs" Moran controlled the North Side. Many men from both sides had been killed in the conflict. Early in 1929, Capone decided to settle the rivalry once and for all. He and his men outlined a bold plan. To establish an alibi, Capone left for a vacation in Florida.

Neighbors who saw a black Cadillac touring car pull up in front of the S.M.C. Cartage Company garage at 2122 North Clark Street at 10:30 on the morning of February 14, 1929, thought they were watching an event then typical in Chicago—a police raid of suspected gang members. The garage was known to be the hangout of Bugs Moran's gang, and Chicago police detectives used cars just like the black Cadillac. And, in fact, three uniformed policemen and two in plain clothes got out of the car and stormed into the garage.

One of the locals who witnessed this scene was Bugs Moran himself. Late to meet his boys after a cup of coffee at a nearby café, he had time to turn on his heel as soon as he saw the Cadillac pull up. Moran quickly ducked into a nearby drugstore. In a few minutes, Moran heard a harsh series of shots ring out.

The "cops" had rounded up the mobsters inside the garage, lined them up facing a brick wall, and shot them all to death with sawed-off shotguns and Thompson submachine guns. It wasn't a police raid—it was a hit by Al Capone. Six of Bugs Moran's top men, the core of his organization, and a hapless optometrist who liked to hang out with them, lay dead: Adam Heyer, Albert Weinshank, John May, James Clark, brothers Pete and Frank Gusenberg, and Dr. Reinhardt Schwimmer. Later, a thoroughly shaken Bugs Moran had only one comment for the police and the press: "Only Capone kills like that!"

The city of Chicago had endured gangland wars for ten years. The average citizen never seemed to get too upset about one mobster killing another, and the police seemed to take the same attitude. But this killing, quickly dubbed the "St. Valentine's Day Massacre," signaled a dramatic rise in the level and intensity of the violence. Who knew what horrors might visit the streets of the city in the future? The public was outraged.

Despite intense public pressure, the police were unable to pin the job on their chief suspects, Capone and his lieutenants. It was widely believed that the job was masterminded by "Machine Gun" Jack McGurn. He, however, produced Louise Rolfe, a woman who insisted that McGurn had been with her on the fateful morning; the press quickly dubbed Rolfe the "Blonde Alibi."

Through ballistics, the police did link one suspect to the crime: Fred R. "Killer" Burke, who fled to Michigan before the Chicago police could nab him. He committed a capital crime inside Michigan and allowed himself to be caught in order to avoid extradition to Chicago. Burke spent the rest of his life in a Michigan prison, thus avoiding police and mob punishment for his role in the Massacre.

This bloodbath put an end to the North Side mob. Bugs Moran eventually turned to bank robbery and died in prison in the late 1950s. For Al Capone, the murders strengthened his grip on Chicago's bootlegging trade but hastened his downfall. Federal investigators, intent upon bringing him to heel, nailed him in 1931 for income-tax evasion. After serving eight years of an 11-year sentence, Capone retired to his Florida estate. He died there of syphilis in 1947.

SAMUEL SHEPPARD

MYSTERY STILL SURROUNDS THE BLUDGEONING DEATH OF MARILYN SHEPPARD.

It began in the wee hours of July 4, 1954. Samuel Sheppard, a handsome, 30-year-old osteopathic surgeon, and his pregnant wife, Marilyn, had been entertaining neighbors in their white frame house on the shore of Lake Erie in the quiet, affluent Cleveland suburb of Bay Village. Sheppard, whom patients and colleagues referred to as "Dr. Sam," had come off a hard day of surgery and had fallen asleep on the living room couch. When the guests left, his wife left him where he was and retired to their upstairs bedroom. There is only Sam Sheppard's version of what occurred during the ensuing five and a half hours.

According to Sheppard, he was awakened in the night by his wife's scream. Rushing upstairs, he charged into their bedroom and was struck from behind while grappling with "a form" wearing a light-colored garment. Sheppard did not know whether he had battled one or two intruders.

In any case, he claimed to have discovered his wife's body when he regained consciousness. He determined that his seven-year-old son, Chip, was asleep in the next room unharmed. Then Sheppard pursued the dimly visible, "bushy-haired" form out of the house to the lakefront, where Sheppard was again knocked out during a struggle.

He awoke lying partially in the water. At first, Sheppard thought he was "the victim of a bizarre dream." But when he again examined his wife, he realized that the night's events had been terrifyingly real. Marilyn Sheppard had been bludgeoned about the face and head; deep vertical lacerations scarred her forehead. Sheppard claimed he then called the first number that came to him—that of Bay Village mayor J. Spencer Houk, who lived three doors away. Both men later agreed that Sheppard said something like: "My God, Spence, get over here quick. I think they've killed Marilyn."

Houk and his wife Esther dressed and rushed to the Sheppard house. After both went upstairs to view the murder scene, Houk called the police, an ambulance, and then Sheppard's brother, Richard.

Sheppard was initially treated as a co-victim— he had a neck injury, purportedly from the beating he took. However, he soon was suspected of being the crime's perpetrator when the police could not find the murder weapon or any fingerprints in the house. The supposition was that Sheppard had used the long span of time before the police were summoned to dispose of the weapon, wipe away any incriminating evidence, and contrive his neck injury.

On July 16, an editorial in the *Cleveland Press*, the city's evening daily, attacked "the tragic mishandling of the Sheppard murder investigation." A banner headline four days later declared that Sheppard was "Getting Away With Murder." The following day, the Bay Village council voted to turn over the case to the Cleveland police. But by then it was already too late for a proper investigation.

Hopelessly out of their league, the Bay Village police had terribly mishandled the crime scene. In their amateurishness, they had even asked the high school football team to link hands and wade into Lake Erie on the remote chance that one of them might step on the murder weapon.

Meanwhile, the Cleveland police seemed interested only in unearthing evidence that implicated Sheppard. They found little until they learned that Sheppard had an affair with Susan Hayes, a former laboratory technician at Bay View Hospital, which was owned by Sheppard and his two older brothers, Richard and Stephen, who were also osteopathic surgeons. Now the police had a motive, even if they lacked concrete proof that Sheppard's account of the murder night was fabricated.

At the trial, Susan Hayes testified that Sheppard had promised to marry her if he were ever able to. The coroner, Samuel Gerber, stated that the missing murder weapon was a medical instrument, although he could not specify its exact nature. Sheppard added to his plight by being a stiff, arrogant witness. His fate, for the moment, was sealed.

On December 21, 1954, after 102 hours of deliberation, a jury in Cleveland, Ohio, found Dr. Samuel Sheppard guilty of bludgeoning to death his pregnant wife Marilyn with an unidentified weapon. However, rather than signifying the end of the landmark case that had electrified the nation, Sheppard's conviction for second-degree murder proved to be only the first chapter in a continuing melodrama.

Sentenced to life in prison by Judge Edward Blythin, Sheppard turned his back, perhaps intentionally, to the jury that had doubted his innocence. The convicted killer then stated, "I'd like to say, sir, that I am not guilty. I feel there has been proof presented to this court that has definitely proved that I couldn't have performed the act charged against me."

Sheppard's protestation was given little credence by anyone except his parents and brothers. Even Judge Blythin was overheard to remark that Sheppard was "guilty as hell." In the following years, however, public sentiment changed and

Sheppard came to be regarded as an innocent man who had been wrongly convicted.

During the ten years Sam Sheppard spent in the Ohio State Penitentiary, he was a model prisoner who volunteered for hazardous medical experiments. Fellow convicts believed he was the rare one among them who was as innocent as he claimed, but the courts denied his appeals for a new trial. Eventually, Erle Stanley Gardner, the creator of Perry Mason, became involved; he wrote of Sheppard's ordeal in his "The Court of Last Resort" column in *Argosy* magazine. Gardner cited Paul Leland Kirk, a criminalistics professor at the University of California, who gave the murder room and many trial exhibits their first, and probably only, thorough scientific examination.

Kirk discovered that the state had suppressed evidence of a blood type found in the murder room that belonged neither to Sheppard nor to his wife. Kirk also found that the killer was probably left-handed—Sheppard was right-handed—and that Marilyn had been slain by many blows delivered over a long period of time and with little force. From this it was surmised that the murderer might be a woman, perhaps the jealous wife of a man with whom Marilyn was having an affair.

In June 1965, Sheppard was granted a new trial, not because new evidence had surfaced, but because the U.S. Supreme Court felt that his right to a fair trial had been violated by prejudicial news coverage.

At the second trial, in late 1966, F. Lee Bailey acted as Sheppard's counsel. Lending Sheppard moral support was Ariane Tebbenjohanns, an attractive European divorcée. She had read of the case in a German magazine and had begun a correspondence with Sheppard that culminated in their marriage when he was released on bail.

The state contended it would easily convict Sheppard a second time. Bailey promised to produce evidence that the real slayer was a woman—Mayor Houk's wife was the leading candidate. However, the high point of the trial was Coroner Gerber's contention that the murder weapon was a medical instrument. But he admitted that in 12 years, he never found an instrument that fit the bloody imprint left on a pillow near Marilyn Sheppard's savagely beaten body.

Found innocent, Sheppard had his medical license restored and moved back to Bay Village. Quickly, though, his new life fell apart. He was sued for divorce by Tebbenjohanns on the grounds of mental cruelty; she claimed he kept a gun on hand believing that someone was out to get him. Socked with two malpractice suits, Sheppard gave up medicine to become a professional wrestler. He then married the young daughter of his wrestling manager and joined a motorcycle gang.

The bizarre story ended in 1970, when Sam Sheppard died of alcohol and drug abuse. Allegedly, he struggled with his last breath to name the person he thought had killed his wife.

The Sheppard murder case remains officially open, and periodic developments still give reason to believe it might one day be solved. In 1982, some old fireplace tongs that were initially thought to be the long-lost murder weapon were found buried in the yard of the house where Mayor Houk and his wife had lived at the time of the crime. During a June 1990 appearance on the *Larry King Show*, Sheppard's son maintained that authorities refuse to investigate an Ohio convict who is strongly suspected of his mother's murder. Two months later, a prominent San Francisco attorney who knew Sheppard and his wife while in high school was mysteriously murdered. Sheppard supporters claim that these developments could lead to the true facts in the murder of Marilyn Sheppard.

PATRICK SHERRILL

HE DIED WITH THE MACABRE DISTINCTION OF HAVING CAUSED THE THIRD-WORST ONE-DAY MASS SLAYING IN THE UNITED STATES.

Patrick Sherrill abhorred his job. To him, carrying letters part time for the Edmond, Oklahoma, post office was merely the latest in a string of loathsome occupations he had held down in the previous 17 years. Perhaps the greatest malcontent of the twentieth century, Sherrill decided to unleash his anger against "the system."

On August 20, 1986, brandishing two .45-caliber pistols and a single .22-caliber weapon, he burst into the post office and declared open season on its employees. Before the melee was over, Sherrill would claim the lives of 14 postal workers before shooting himself to death. Sherrill died with the macabre distinction of having caused the third-worst one-day mass slaying in the United States.

When Sherrill and his arsenal arrived at the post office that day, the building was not yet open to the public. Inside, 90 postal workers were preparing for a day of business. Sherrill shot randomly for 40 minutes, killing and maiming postal workers who were sorting mail, other employees who were enjoying their morning coffee and doughnuts—anyone whose misfortune it was to be within the letter carrier's range. Initially, postal workers mistook Sherrill's gunfire for firecrackers ignited as a prank. They realized their mistake when they saw a fellow worker lying in a pool of blood. They fled for their lives. Fortunately, some of those inside the building managed to escape Sherrill's mayhem.

Police officers found 13 bodies inside the new, one-story building and another outside the rear doors. During an unsuccesful attempt to negotiate with Sherrill, officers heard two shots, one of which Sherrill apparently fired at his head.

Sherrill, 44, was basically a loner. He was a bicycling enthusiast and was also interested in ham radio. A former marine, guns were his true passion. He collected several of them. He was an expert marksman, as he proved on the morning of September 23.

Postal employees told officers that Sherrill, on the verge of being fired, had said "his supervisor was going to pay for what he was doing." Sherrill's revenge was bloody, and it ended in his own death.

GEORGE JOSEPH SMITH

ALWAYS A BRIDEGROOM, SMITH MARRIED WOMEN WITH AN UNFORTUNATE PROPENSITY FOR MISADVENTURE IN THE BATH.

George Joseph Smith was not what you would call a talented entrepreneur. Although he did try his hand at running a junk shop and antique dealing, he was never good enough at either to make a great deal of money. Tired of moving from town to town in southern England, he decided to hone the one talent that he did have—finding wives.

George married Caroline Thornhill in 1898. The marriage lasted only two years, and she left him by 1900 without ever divorcing him. That mere technicality did not stop George from marrying again. Calling himself Henry Williams, he married his second wife, Beatrice Mundy, in 1910. She was a 33-year-old woman with a sizable bank account, which turned out to interest George more than his wife. He left Beatrice that same year, only to marry her again two years later.

After he and Beatrice set up house for the second

time in 1912, Smith had a new bathtub installed. Soon, he was complaining to his doctor that his wife was having fits. Even before the doctor arrived to examine poor Beatrice, she died. When the doctor finally examined her naked body in the water-filled bathtub, he called the death an accident. Smith appeared to be overcome with grief, finding solace playing "Nearer My God to Thee" on his harmonium.

Still bitten by the marrying bug, Smith proceeded to audition a number of new bridal prospects, finally choosing Alice Burnham of Bristol. She had £500 in her bank account and, like her predecessor, an unfortunate propensity for misadventure in the bath. Although at least one neighbor was unconvinced of Smith's innocence in Alice's death, he remained free and unsuspected by the police.

On December 17, 1914, using the name John Lloyd, Smith married Margaret Elizabeth Lofty. On the very next day, Margaret Elizabeth went to a watery death in her bath. The coroner brought in another verdict of misadventure, and the bereaved husband pocketed £700. This death, however, was front-page news that brought forth people who remembered what had happened to Beatrice Mundy and Alice Burnham. On the testimony of Alice Burnham's father and landlady, Smith was arrested.

George Joseph Smith was first charged with

bigamy. After further investigation, murder was added to the charge. Smith was defended by Edward Marshall Hall, a very good barrister who could do nothing to refute damning forensic evidence. It was the simple but elegant testimony of Scotland Yard's Bernard Spilsbury that sealed Smith's fate. Spilsbury said that each of the women was too tall to have simply slipped under the water. Force had to have been applied. A courtroom demonstration of Smith's probable method of murder nearly resulted in the drowning death of the woman who had agreed to participate in the reenactment. This dramatic moment is what convinced the jury of Smith's guilt. Later, as the jury received final instructions from the judge, Smith lept to his feet and shouted, "I am not a murderer, though I may be a bit peculiar!" By that time, few in the courtroom were inclined to disagree with the latter part of his statement.

George Joseph Smith was hanged on Friday the 13th in August 1915. After his death, yet another bride turned up, a living one named Edith Pegler, who had married Smith in 1908. She told the authorities that her husband would disappear at intervals, but would return to her at times that coincided with the aftermath of each "misadventure." So clever was the smooth-talking Smith that Edith had been unaware of his deadly avocation during their marriage.

SON OF SAM
DAVID BERKOWITZ

"YOU FINALLY GOT ME," HE SAID. "I GUESS THIS IS THE END OF THE TRAIL."

The "Son of Sam" who terrorized New York in the 1970s with his killing spree was born David Richard Berkowitz in Brooklyn on June 1, 1953. His mother, who was unmarried, gave him up for adoption. Many years later, psychiatrists who examined him theorized that the trauma of being rejected by his mother led Berkowitz to develop the violent hatreds that he showed as "Son of Sam."

Though Berkowitz's intelligence was above average, he suffered from desperately low self-esteem. He became a prolific arsonist as a teenager. Though he got a decent job with the U.S. Postal Service, his morale did not improve. He became increasingly withdrawn, a paranoid loner.

Eventually Berkowitz's depressed mental state and low self-esteem developed into a hatred for women. Berkowitz acted on this hatred in his crimes. Twice in December 1975, Berkowitz committed knife attacks against women. Both victims survived.

Berkowitz then exchanged his knife for a powerful .44-caliber Bulldog revolver. On the night of July 29, 1976, he used this weapon to shoot Donna Lauria and Jody Valenti in a parked car. Lauria was killed, and Valenti was seriously wounded.

Berkowitz struck again on October 23, 1976. Attacking, as always, at night, he shot at Carl Denaro and Rosemary Keenan in a parked car in Flushing, New York. Denaro suffered a crippling wound to one of his fingers; Keenan was unhurt. On November 26, Berkowitz shot Donna DeMasi and Joanne Lomino on the front stoop of a house in Queens. Neither was killed, but DeMasi was paralyzed from her waist down.

By then, panic over the shootings gripped the metropolitan New York City area. The search for the elusive killer involved hundreds of police and detectives and eventually led to the formation of a multiunit task force. The pursuit of the ".44-caliber killer," as he was initially called, became the greatest manhunt in the city's history.

On January 30, 1977, Berkowitz shot and killed Christine Freund in a parked car in New York's Ridgewood neighborhood. On March 8, he murdered Virginia Voskerian in Forest Hills.

On April 17, his .44 claimed the lives of Alexander Esau and Valentina Suriani, both shot in the same parked car in the Bronx. This time, he left a message to his pursuers that gave him his sobriquet. At the scene of the crime, Berkowitz dropped a letter in which he explained that his orders to kill had come from barking dogs that were actually demons. A certain dog named Sam was possessed by his father's evil spirit; hence, he signed the letter "Son of Sam." In subsequent letters to police and to newspaper columnist Jimmy Breslin, the Son of Sam taunted his pursuers and warned of future attacks.

He was as good as his word. On June 26, 1977, he shot and wounded Salvatore Lupo and Judy Placido in a parked car in Queens. On July 31, he shot Stacy Moskowitz and Robert Violante in a parked car in Brooklyn. Moskowitz later died; Violante was partially blinded.

This last shooting led to a break in the case. A woman walking her dog near the crime scene saw policemen ticketing an illegally parked Ford Galaxy. A few minutes later, she saw a man hurriedly drive off in the same car. She reported all this to the police, who traced the ticket to Berkowitz.

Berkowitz was arrested outside his Yonkers apartment building on August 10, 1977. He submitted amiably to the arresting officer, Inspector Dowd. "You finally got me," he told Dowd. "I guess this is the end of the trail." It certainly was.

The prosecution had an airtight case against David Berkowitz. He pleaded not guilty by reason of insanity, but the jury rejected that defense after psychiatrists testified that he was faking his disorder. The Son of Sam was ultimately sentenced to a total of 365 years at the Attica Correctional Facility in upstate New York, where he remains to this day.

RICHARD SPECK

THE HELL-RAISER KILLED EIGHT STUDENT NURSES: A NINTH ONE SAVED HER LIFE BY HIDING.

Born in Illinois in 1941, Richard Franklin Speck was a battered child who grew up to be a drunk and a drug user. He had the reputation of being a hell-raiser on his various jobs as a hand on Great Lakes freighters. Speck often moved between Texas and Illinois and had quite an arrest record in both states. He was busted 37 times for a variety of crimes. His tattoo: "Born to Raise Hell" was an accurate portrayal of his life, as psychologists believed that his many head injuries as a child left him incapable of judging right from wrong.

Speck could not get a job on a ship bound to New Orleans on the night of July 13-14, 1966. Frustrated and drunk, the 25-year-old was looking for trouble as he walked along east 100th Street on Chicago's South Side. Across the street from Luella Public Elementary School, he knocked on the door of townhouse 2319. Corazon Amurao, a 23-year-old student nurse, opened the door. Speck flashed a gun and a knife as he pushed his way inside. At the time he assured the frightened young woman that he would not hurt her—a promise that he did not intend to keep.

Speck ordered her upstairs, where he found five more women—three in one bedroom, two in another. He commanded the student nurses to lie on the floor in one of the bedrooms. Then he ripped a bed sheet into strips, which he used to tie up each student. Speck again promised his prisoners that he would not harm them.

At 11:30 P.M., Gloria Davy, 22, returned home. Speck directed her upstairs to join the others. He bound her without delay. Suzanne Farris, 21, arrived after midnight with 20-year-old Mary Ann Jordan, a guest for the night. Speck also tied them up. He announced, "I need your money to go to New Orleans." He rifled through their purses, wallets, and dressers.

Apparently in a muddled state, Speck sat on the floor toying with his gun. He then untied Pamela Wilkening, 20, and took her to an adjacent bedroom. Speck plunged his knife into her left breast and strangled her. Mary Ann Jordan and Suzanne Farris were seized next and pushed into a third bedroom. He killed Jordan with stabs to her neck, breast, and eye. Farris tried to fight off the knife-wielding attacker, but he overpowered her, driving the knife into her 18 times. After she collapsed, he strangled her. He then ripped off her underclothing and tore them to shreds.

Speck took time to wash his hands before returning to his march of murder. In sequence, he killed Nina Schmale, 23; Valentina Pasion, 23; Marlita Gargullo, 23; and Patricia Matusek, 20. All were stabbed, strangled, or both. During this sequence, Amurao hid herself under a bed. Speck had apparently lost count of the number of women in the townhouse, and he never found Amurao.

From her position under the bed, Amurao watched Speck pull off Gloria Davy's jeans before raping her. Speck then took his final victim downstairs, and sodomized and killed her. Amurao, frozen with fear, remained cowering under the bed for hours.

After he left the townhouse, Speck shuffled along skid row on Chicago's Madison Street, barhopping. He drank incessantly for three days and spent three dollars on a prostitute.

Corazon Amurao's detailed information led to Speck's arrest. He was tried in the spring of 1967. After deliberating for 49 minutes, the jury found Speck guilty of murder and sentenced him to death. When the U.S. Supreme Court abolished capital punishment, Speck escaped the electric chair. He was resentenced in 1972 to a series of life terms totaling hundreds of years.

CHARLES STARKWEATHER

IN ONE MEMORABLE MONTH, HE WENT ON A MURDER RAMPAGE SO INTENSE THE NATIONAL GUARD WAS CALLED TO HELP IN HIS CAPTURE.

In 1957, Charles Starkweather, 19, worked as a garbageman in Lincoln, Nebraska. He was born poor, but he had bigger plans for himself. He idolized the movie star James Dean and had images of himself standing up to the authorities in the same way Dean's screen characters did.

The little garbageman robbed a gas station on December 1, 1957. He then drove station attendant Robert Colvert to an isolated spot and killed him. Nearly two months later, he started his killing spree in earnest.

On January 28, 1958, Starkweather was at the home of his 14-year-old girlfriend, Caril Ann Fugate, waiting for her to arrive from school. With him was his constant companion, a .22-caliber rifle. Starkweather got into an argument with Caril Ann's parents, Velda and Marion Bartlett. He fired his rifle at Mr. Bartlett, who was killed. Starkweather then proceeded to murder Caril Ann's mother. Caril Ann arrived home in time to see her boyfriend choke her stepsister, Betty Jean, to death with his rifle. Caril Ann thought fast and scribbled a note saying that the entire family had the flu and that everyone should stay away. She tacked the note to the front door of the house and made herself at home with Charles.

As if nothing had happened, the unabashed couple made sandwiches, watched TV, and necked on the sofa. The note kept anyone who was suspicious away at first, but the police were soon alerted.

Before the police arrived, Starkweather and Caril Ann had driven Charles's hot rod to parts unknown. When the carnage was discovered, an alert went out across Nebraska, Kansas, South Dakota, and Wyoming to look out for Charles Starkweather.

The villainous couple stopped at the farm of August Meyer. Starkweather and Caril Ann left Meyer for dead. Next, they came across another teenaged couple. Seventeen-year-old Robert Jensen was shot; 16-year-old Carol King was shot after being raped.

Charles and Caril Ann drove back into the Lincoln suburbs and selected a wealthy household at random. C. Lauer Ward, president of Capital Steel Works; his wife, Clara; and their maid, Lillian Fenci, were bound and gagged. The victims remained alive while Starkweather and Caril Ann helped themselves to food and other goodies. Eventually, however, Starkweather began to mutilate his helpless victims with a knife. Finally, he ended their torment by killing them.

By this time, a 1,200-man posse, backed by a troop of the National Guard, was forming a dragnet for Starkweather and Caril Ann. In Douglas, Wyoming, the young lovers shot shoe salesman Merle Collison. When they tried to get away, their car wouldn't start. Starkweather asked a passerby, oil agent Joseph Sprinkle, for help. The alert Sprinkle grabbed Starkweather's rifle and held him at bay while the police were called. As Caril Ann eagerly surrendered herself (she had grown tired of the "adventure"), Starkweather managed to escape in Sprinkle's car. During the chase, he was grazed by a police bullet. His minor wound frightened him; he stopped the car and was captured. Starkweather's rampage had lasted 26 days.

Tried and convicted, Starkweather went to his death a boastfully proud killer. He died in the Nebraska electric chair on June 24, 1959.

Caril Ann Fugate denied any complicity in the crimes and swore that she was kidnapped. No one believed her. Although a minor, she was sentenced to life in prison. She continued to protest her innocence and was paroled in 1977.

JOEL STEINBERG

JOEL STEINBERG BEAT HIS SIX-YEAR-OLD "ADOPTED" DAUGHTER TO DEATH WITH HIS BARE HANDS.

A parade of witnesses, including police, doctors, and neighbors, couldn't tell jurors as much about the savagery as the silent testimony of pictures. The visual record of abuse and the testimony of her "adoptive" mother spoke volumes for six-year-old Lisa Steinberg, who could no longer speak for herself. The pretty girl with hazel eyes and shoulder-length hair had been brutally beaten to death by lawyer Joel Steinberg.

Years of abuse culminated on November 2, 1987, as Lisa lay comatose and naked on the bathroom floor of a Greenwich Village apartment. Hedda Nussbaum, Joel Steinberg's common-law wife, dialed the 911 emergency phone number, and stated that Lisa had stopped breathing.

Officers responding from New York City's Sixth Precinct and paramedics from St. Vincent's Hospital were revolted by the condition of the apartment. The place was filthy, foul-smelling, dark, and cluttered with broken chairs and furniture; it was far below acceptable living conditions. The media later dubbed it "the Cave." Emergency attempts to revive the child failed, and she was rushed to the hospital. The attending physician found severe beating trauma to Lisa's head and body and immediately suspected brain damage. Despite all attempts to save her, Lisa was dead, a victim of child abuse.

The investigation following Lisa's death revealed Steinberg's shady past. He had somehow bypassed the New York bar examination. His mob connections led to drug abuse, that eventually grew to free-basing cocaine nightly. Steinberg violently beat Hedda Nussbaum and virtually controlled her life from the time they met in 1975. Steinberg enrolled her in his lifestyle of drug abuse, and drug addiction took control of both their lives.

Another aspect of Steinberg's devious past concerned his illegal adoption of Lisa. Steinberg took possession of baby Lisa when the biological mother—young and unmarried—released her child to Steinberg after he promised to place the baby with Catholic parents. When the recipient parents failed to pay his illegal $50,000 fee, Steinberg kept the baby and had thugs beat up the parents.

Hedda Nussbaum, addicted to drugs and trying to care for Lisa, was frequently absent from her job as an editor and unable to perform her job whenever she did go to work. Eventually, Nussbaum was fired. Steinberg's increasing drug abuse led to more frequent and severe beatings of Nussbaum and attacks to her self-esteem. Steinberg ruptured Nussbaum's spleen, smashed her nose, gave her a cauliflower ear, knocked out several teeth, fractured nine ribs, and broke her jaw. He also burned her face, leaving her grotesquely scarred. Attempts by Nussbaum's family and friends to help her were thwarted by Steinberg.

Although Nussbaum's appearance told the story of her horrible life with Steinberg, the focus of the investigation centered on Lisa. Steinberg had literally beaten a defenseless child to death. Early reports stated that he had beaten Lisa with an exercise bar, but that was later corrected: He had beaten her "with his bare hands."

Steinberg was arrested on a murder charge. On October 17, 1988, the trial began in a Manhattan courtroom before Judge Harold J. Rothwax. The prosecution's case included visual records and Nussbaum's testimony, which detailed Lisa's injuries and her lying unconscious for hours before help was summoned.

Steinberg was found guilty of manslaughter in the first degree. He was sentenced to $8^1/2$ to 25 years in the Dannemora State Prison with a recommendation of no parole.

CHARLES STUART

RACIAL TENSIONS FLARED WHEN BOSTON POLICE SEARCHED FOR THE AFRICAN AMERICAN THAT CHARLES STUART CLAIMED KILLED HIS WIFE.

When the dispatcher for the 911 emergency phone number answered the call, a voice at the other end painfully gasped, "My wife's been shot. I've been shot." It was the night of October 23, 1989, and Charles Stuart was calling from his car phone, but he was unable to give the location of his car.

When Boston police finally reached the scene, they found Stuart, 29, shot in the abdomen. His pregnant wife, 30-year-old Carol, lay unconscious from a severe head wound. Rushed to a nearby hospital, Charles survived but Carol did not. Delivered by cesarean section, baby son Christopher outlived his mother by only 17 days.

Charles Stuart told police that he and Carol, both white, were returning home from a childbirth class when they were stopped by an African-American man. Stuart said that the man forced them to drive to an isolated area before he shot and robbed them.

Racial tensions flared in Boston as police indiscriminately detained more than 200 African-American men who fit the gunman's description. Stuart identified one of those arrested in a lineup, but no formal charges were filed. Eventually, the investigators suspected Stuart himself, who had collected an insurance payment of $82,000 only three days after the shootings.

The investigators' suspicions were confirmed when Stuart's brother Matthew told police that Charles had given him Carol's handbag to throw into the Pines River. The bag was recovered along with a .38-caliber revolver that had been reported missing from a safe in Kakas & Sons furriers, which Charles had managed.

Although it had then become clear to the authorities that Stuart had shot himself and murdered his wife for the money, he was neither charged nor brought to trial. Instead, on January 4, 1990, approximately three months after his wife's death, an apparently guilt-tormented Charles Stuart committed suicide by jumping into the Mystic River.

PETER SUTCLIFFE
THE YORKSHIRE RIPPER

WHEN HE PULLED UP THE PROSTITUTE'S CLOTHES AND STABBED HER BREAST AND ABDOMEN, HE WAS LITERALLY COMMITTING RAPE WITH A KNIFE.

Born in Yorkshire, England, on June 2, 1946, Peter Sutcliffe was the oldest of five children and his mother's favorite. A lonely, shy boy, he left school at 15 and drifted from one job to another. When he was 21, he began dating a 16-year-old Czech girl named Sonia Szurma, and seven years later they married.

One night Sonia was out on a date with someone else. Intensely jealous, Sutcliffe went to a prostitute, but he failed to have intercourse. The prostitute taunted and humiliated him and took his money without returning his change. At that moment, he felt a hatred toward prostitutes that remained with him and soon festered into murderous feelings.

In 1969, Sutcliffe made his first attack on a prostitute—he hit her on the head with a sock filled with gravel. Two years later, he was on a drive with a friend in a red-light district when he hit another woman with a brick enclosed in a sock.

The year after he married Sonia, Sutcliffe escalated his long, vengeful reign of terror by hitting and slashing two prostitutes. A few months later, he committed his first murder in Leeds. In the wee hours of October 29, 1975, Sutcliffe struck hooker Wilma McCann on the head with a hammer. When he pulled up her clothes and stabbed her breast and abdomen, he was literally committing rape with a knife; it gave Sutcliffe an unexpected sexual thrill.

Sutcliffe seemed to concentrate on prostitutes. Emily Jackson was a mother of three who earned extra money by soliciting while her husband was at work. She was found dead on January 21, 1976. Her chest had been stabbed at least 50 times and her head battered with a hammer.

A year passed before Sutcliffe killed again, but during 1977 he attacked repeatedly. On February 5, a jogger found Irene Richardson in a park in Leeds with her throat slashed. On April 23, prostitute Tina Anderson was found dead in her bed. Though she had not been raped, she had been the victim of what the police called a "frenzied sexual attack." On June 25, 16-year-old Jayne MacDonald—who was not a prostitute at all, but an innocent shopgirl—was found beaten with Sutcliffe's hammer and stabbed repeatedly. On October 10, Jean Royle's body was found in a cemetery in Manchester. She had been dead since October 1. The violence of the attack on her body surpassed anything Sutcliffe had done before. Her head had been repeatedly bashed in with a hammer, and her stomach had been ripped open. Furthermore, he had apparently come back to her body days later to continue his mutilation.

But Jean Royle's death provided police with a clue. A £5 note in her purse was traced to Sutcliffe's workplace. In fact, he was questioned about the murders and released.

Sutcliffe showed on April 4, 1979, that he was willing to attack women other than prostitutes. Josephine Whitaker, 19, was walking home from a visit with her grandmother when Sutcliffe attacked her. He fractured her skull and stabbed her with a rusty screwdriver that he had sharpened especially for the purpose.

In all, Sutcliffe hammered and mutilated 14 women, three of whom survived. His last victim, attacked on November 17, 1980, was 20-year-old Jacqueline Hill, a Leeds University student.

The hunt for the murderer now known as the Yorkshire Ripper had become one of the most extensive police operations in English history. Hundreds of thousands of interviews had been conducted. More than 30,000 written statements had been taken. A special force of England's six top police detectives was created to find the Ripper. Even the FBI offered help. On January 2, 1981, while routinely checking license plates, Sergeant Robert Ring and Police Constable Robert Hydes arrested Sutcliffe as he picked up a prostitute. When they suspected his identity after finding a ball-headed hammer and a knife that he had hidden, Sutcliffe admitted that he was the Yorkshire Ripper. Found guilty on May 22, 1981, Peter Sutcliffe was jailed for life.

WILLIAM DESMOND TAYLOR

WHEN A HOLLYWOOD DIRECTOR WAS MURDERED, THE SCRIPT CALLED FOR A COVER-UP.

On February 2, 1922, William Desmond Taylor, the famous and well-respected movie director, was found murdered in his Hollywood bungalow. Within minutes following Taylor's death, phones all over Hollywood began to ring. People in the know wanted certain facts about the killing hushed up. By the time the police arrived, studio executives were burning papers in the bungalow's fireplace; the houseboy was in the kitchen washing evidence from the dishes; and (it was rumored) comedy star Mabel Normand was searching the place for her love letters. Several unidentified people also were on the scene, and some of them were rumored to be drug dealers.

The bungalow was in utter chaos, when an unidentified doctor arrived to sign Taylor's death certificate. He examined the body and pronounced Taylor dead from a stomach hemorrhage. When men from the coroner's office lifted the body to put it on a litter, they discovered blood on the floor and a bullet hole in Taylor's back. The cause of death obviously wasn't a stomach hemorrhage; it was murder, plain and simple.

In Hollywood nothing is ever simple. The police had not rushed to Taylor's bungalow to investigate a murder because they had been called by one of the studios—Paramount—and told that the whole matter was a sensitive one. Hollywood in 1922 was very much a company town, and the movie studios controlled the police. In this case the police accepted Paramount's word that nothing was amiss. By the time the police realized that they'd been hoodwinked, it was too late to seal off the crime scene or properly collect crucial evidence.

Reporters from all parts of the United States quickly descended on the crime scene. They dished out gossip and spun out innuendos, staying around long enough to ruin the careers of several famous actresses. But they were too late. By the time they had arrived, the truth had already gone with the wind.

The exact facts that Paramount wanted to cover up have never been determined. It was known that William Desmond Taylor was the studio's star director and its greatest creative talent. And it was common knowledge that Taylor worked with Paramount's biggest stars: Mabel Normand and young, pretty Mary Miles Minter, the 15-year-old budding actress who seemed to have a promising future as a leading lady. Indeed, women figured prominently in Taylor's life. It was rumored that a large assemblage of pornographic photos was found in the bungalow, along with a collection of lingerie that had been tagged with dates and initials, as if they were gaming trophies. Love letters were also found—not from Mabel Normand, but from young Mary Minter. The letters allegedly confirmed that the 54-year-old Taylor had been carrying on a torrid affair with Minter.

Investigation into the director's life revealed several unknown facets: The highly respected William Desmond Taylor was actually William Deane Tanner, husband of retired actress Ethel May Harrison and co-owner of a posh New York antique store. Between the time of his New York society life and his Hollywood celebrity life, he had been a timekeeper for the Yukon Gold Company in Alaska; a night clerk at the Inter Ocean Hotel in Cheyenne, Wyoming; a gold prospector in Colorado; and an acclaimed theatrical performer in San Francisco.

As intriguing as Taylor's past was, it couldn't compete with the list of suspects in his murder. Charlotte Selby, Mary Miles Minter's dominating mother, had threatened to kill Taylor if he didn't end his affair with her daughter. Taylor's close friend Mabel Normand, a gifted but fading star, was rumored to be hopelessly addicted to morphine. There is speculation that Taylor's efforts to save Normand from her addiction got him into trouble with drug-dealing underworld figures. One of Taylor's ex-employees had stolen from him and possibly tried to blackmail him to avoid prosecution. Also, the director's houseboy had recently been arrested for soliciting young men in a park. Taylor was to have testified on the houseboy's behalf the day he was murdered.

Most of the rumors that swirled around the front pages in the days following February 2 were generated by Paramount Pictures. Since the rumors had the effect of defaming the studio's former star director, and of ruining the careers of Normand and Minter, one might wonder about what greater secret the studio was trying so hard to cover up. Many writers and amateur investigators have attempted to solve this mystery. Some speculate that Taylor had committed criminal acts in a previous life; others believe that the director was a homosexual in a Hollywood that was loath to deal with one more scandal. There is a wealth of evidence to study—newspaper accounts, police reports, eyewitness testimony. In the end, there is too much evidence and too little fact. That William Desmond Taylor was a man with a mysterious past is a certainty, but the people who knew the truth about his life and death are dead and gone.

HOWARD UNRUH

THE EX-SOLDIER, COLLEGE STUDENT, AND BIBLE SCHOLAR WENT ON A MURDEROUS RAMPAGE AND KILLED 13 INNOCENT PEOPLE.

Howard Unruh certainly seemed like a well-adjusted and pleasant young man. An ex-GI with a sterling war record, he was a serious university student interested in the Bible. On the surface, it seemed that this ex-soldier was a perfectly happy young man. Not until it was too late did anyone realize that Unruh had some deadly serious problems.

Born in 1921, Howard Unruh entered the Army in 1941 as a volunteer, where he developed a reputation as an excellent sharpshooter and tank gunner. After his release from the Army, he quietly settled down to civilian life in Camden, New Jersey. Unruh enrolled in the state university to study pharmacy and attended Bible classes. Looking back, it was odd that this young man showed no interest in socializing and spent most of his free time alone either reading the Bible or studying. As time went on, however, his isolation became more and more pronounced. Unruh developed serious hatred for many people and compiled hate lists of neighbors whose behavior annoyed him. He even made notations of which people he would like to get back at with the word "retal," meaning that these people were marked for retaliation.

Then his behavior grew more overtly troubled. His interest in weapons was reignited. He began collecting high-powered weapons and putting in long hours of target practice. He went so far as to erect a heavy fence around his backyard to protect his "secrets" and keep out intruders. Unruh labored long and hard to create an armor-plated gate for his fortress. It was an imposing gate, but since it rested on simple, exposed hinges, it must have proved to be an irresistible target for a neighborhood prank, because it was soon removed.

On September 5, 1949, when Unruh discovered his gate missing, he lost control of the delicate balance that had held his life together. He decided the time had come for "massive retal." His first target might have been his mother, but she noticed the crazed look in his eyes at breakfast, so she quickly left. She ran to a neighbor's house, but unfortunately, she did not call the police immediately. Meanwhile, Unruh armed himself with a 9mm Luger and another pistol, then filled his pockets with ammunition. At 9:20 A.M., the crazed ex-GI walked out of his house and down the street, shooting randomly at everyone he saw. His prowess as a marksman was such that few who came into his sights were spared. Amazingly, 13 people were shot to death in only 12 minutes.

Unruh returned to his house and barricaded himself in his bedroom. As police arrived and surrounded the house, he answered a telephone call from a local newspaper. He talked to them calmly and rationally, but then tear gas came through the window and he hung up. Eventually he walked out of the house and surrendered to the police.

Howard Unruh never went to trial. The State of New Jersey sent him directly to the insane asylum—for life. He made only one statement at his commitment hearing: "I'd have killed a thousand if I'd had bullets enough."

JEANNE WEBER

AT FIRST, EVERYONE WAS CONVINCED THE DEATHS WERE NATURAL. AFTER ALL, INFANT MORTALITY IN THE SLUMS OF PARIS WAS HIGH.

Jeanne Weber was born in 1875 in France. She was the daughter of a poor Normandy fisherman, but her family's coastal fishing life did not appeal to her. In 1889, she began working as a maidservant, but domestic service did not suit her either. She began to travel around France picking up what jobs she could. She came to live in Paris in 1893 and eventually met Marcel Weber. They married and had three children.

The Webers found life in the slums of Paris difficult, and both took to drinking heavily to forget their troubles. Both their daughters died suddenly, causing Jeanne to drink even more.

When two small boys for whom she was caring died soon afterward, no one said anything about the matter. After all, infant mortality in the slums of Paris was high. However, there was more con-

cern about an incident that occurred shortly thereafter. Jeanne was looking after the two daughters
of Pierre Weber, one of Marcel's brothers. A neighbor noticed one of the girls, Georgette, apparently
having a fit while sitting on her aunt Jeanne's lap.
The concerned neighbor questioned Jeanne and
was told that everything was fine. Satisfied, the
neighbor left. An hour later, Jeanne reported that
the fit had recurred and the child was dead.

After only nine days, Suzanne, Pierre's other
daughter, was found dead, with a scarf draped
about her neck. Seeing strange marks on the necks
of both children, the doctor refused to sign Suzanne's death certificate. He was overruled by the
police and their official surgeon. They were convinced that the deaths were from natural causes.

The curious incidents continued. Yet another
niece died after three choking episodes, the first
two of which were fortunately interrupted by a vis-
itor. Marcel Weber, Jeanne's own seven-year-old
son, died next. Then Maurice Weber, a nephew,
was left with Jeanne while his mother went shopping. When his mother returned earlier than
expected, she found her son blue-faced and choking. He was rushed to the hospital, where he was
revived. This time the police were called in. The
infants' corpses were exhumed, but by now no
throat marks were discernible. Jeanne was defended by a top lawyer who obtained an acquittal.

Once free, Jeanne Weber left her husband and his now-hostile family. She apparently disappeared—only to emerge again on April 16, 1907. At that time, nine-year-old Auguste Bavouzet died of strangulation at his home in central France. His sister, who disliked their new housekeeper Madame Moulinet, checked her belongings. In Madame's bag, Auguste's sister found damning letters and press clippings—Madame Moulinet was in reality Jeanne Weber. Again, Jeanne was tried and once more acquitted.

Afterward, a Madame Bouchery and her alleged husband checked into an inn in northern France. The woman asked the innkeeper if Marcel, his seven-year-old son, could stay in her room overnight. Madame Bouchery wanted some company while her husband was away at work. Obligingly, the kindly innkeeper gave his approval. Later, the child's screams brought his father running. Unfortunately, the boy's frantic father did not arrive in time. The police appeared, and Madame Bouchery proved to be Jeanne Weber. As Madame Bouchery, she had recently been fired from a children's home where she had been found strangling a sick youngster.

In 1908, Jeanne Weber was declared insane and sent to an asylum. The madwoman died a most appropriate death in 1910, foaming at the mouth, when she strangled herself.

CHARLES JOSEPH WHITMAN

HATRED FOR HIS FATHER SEEMS TO BE THE MOTIVE FOR CHARLES WHITMAN'S KILLING SPREE THAT TOOK 15 LIVES.

Charles Joseph Whitman was a 25-year-old architecture student at the University of Texas at Austin. At about noon on August 1, 1966, he transported a footlocker containing weapons into the 300-foot-high tower of the main campus building. Methodically, he took the elevator up to the 27th floor and carried the footlocker up the remaining three half-flights of stairs to the observation deck. His first victim was the 47-year-old receptionist, Edna Townsley, whom he clubbed to death, hiding her body behind a couch. The young couple who were on the observation deck were luckier—they entered the reception area, said hello to Whitman, and left.

Finally alone, Whitman unpacked his weapons, only to be again interrupted by six unsuspecting tourists. Angrily, he opened fire on them, killing two—Mark Gabour and Margaret Lamport—and injuring two others. Whitman then blocked the door with furniture, carried the weapons onto the observatory walkway, and began to shoot victims up to 500 yards away. His killing spree continued for 90 minutes, during which time he killed ten more people, including an unborn child.

Stopping Whitman's deadly rampage proved to be no easy task for three Austin police officers and a deputized civilian. They had to crawl over bodies on the stairway just to get up to the observation level. Forcing their way into the reception area, the four men stationed themselves outdoors on the observation deck and hid in order to avoid the heavy gunfire by police from below. They trapped Whitman in a corner by coming at him from two directions. Officer Jerry Day and 40-year-old civilian Allen Crum teamed up. As Crum moved along the building's south side to fire a blind shot, Day backed him. The two other officers—Ramiro Martinez, 29, and Houston McCoy, 26—fired at Whitman from the northeast side. Although Officer Martinez's shots missed, Whitman did swing his rifle around to return fire. At this point, McCoy hit him with two shotgun blasts to the head and neck, and Martinez grabbed McCoy's shotgun. Whitman was still moving, but Martinez put an end to his life. At 1:24 P.M., he fired at point-blank range into Whitman, ending this murderous rampage.

Whitman was identified from papers on his body. Police rushed to Whitman's home, looked for his wife, and then went to his mother's apartment. Whitman had murdered both women the night before. The death toll was 15.

That an ordinary college student with ordinary friends and relatives could suddenly become a cold and methodical killer stunned the nation. Acquaintances knew Whitman as an all-American boy; an Eagle Scout at age 12; a former altar boy; and a Scoutmaster.

But Whitman was consumed with hatred for his father—a rigid disciplinarian who beat his children and wife. Whitman's mother had left his father a few months earlier; this seemed to revive Whitman's recurring battles with violent impulses. Whitman visited the school psychiatrist, mentioning these impulses and an urge to go "up on the tower with a deer rifle and start shooting people."

During an investigation, police found letters written by Whitman. They told of Whitman's hatred for his father and his love for his wife and mother. Whitman felt he could no longer control himself and did not want to leave his wife and mother to suffer the consequences of the horrible thing he had to do. In one note, Whitman had asked for an autopsy to determine if he had any mental disorders. A walnut-size tumor was discovered, but its effects are disputed.

CHRISTOPHER WILDER

HE BEGAN AN ODYSSEY OF TERROR THAT EXTENDED FROM FLORIDA TO CALIFORNIA AND BACK TO NEW HAMPSHIRE.

Christopher Wilder seemed to have it all: looks, money, friends, a career. Unfortunately, he also had deranged sexual cravings that he was unable to control.

Born in 1945 in Australia, Wilder had an Australian mother and a U.S. Navy man for a father. His father was stationed in the United States at the end of the war, where young Christopher was raised. Although he was bright, Wilder dropped out of school and returned to Australia. He fell deeply in love. That relationship ended, badly, and he wed on the rebound. His marriage was later annulled.

A good-looking surfer, Wilder found it easy to pick up women. He had long-term relationships with women who resembled his early love. However, Wilder also had a secret sex life that began during his teens—a "game" in which he pretended to be a modeling agent in order to have sex with pretty young women. Once he was arrested for participating in a gang rape. His sentence included electroshock treatments, which he later used on his victims. After returning to the United States, Wilder continued with his secret games. Tried for rape in 1977, he was acquitted.

By 1984, Wilder was a wealthy 39-year-old playboy contractor with an attractive home in Boynton Beach, Florida. He had a good reputation and many friends. However, his secret sexual obsession had worsened. He fantasized about violence and domination, and he had trouble perceiving where his fantasies ended.

Accused of kidnapping two models, Beth Kenyon and Rosario Gonzales, in March 1984, Wilder began an odyssey of terror that extended from Florida to California and back to New Hampshire. Despite being on the FBI's Most Wanted List and the target of the biggest manhunt since Dillinger, Wilder continued to lure aspiring models until April. He allegedly kidnapped, sexually tortured, and/or killed at least 12 women. Three lived; two were never found.

On April 13, 1984, Wilder had almost reached the Canadian border in New Hampshire. He accidentally killed himself while trying to shoot a highway patrolman who was struggling with him.

WAYNE WILLIAMS

HIS ARREST PUT AN END TO THE MURDERS OF BLACK CHILDREN IN ATLANTA.

In early 1981, after more than a dozen Atlanta-area black youths were murdered, the national media focused on the efforts to find the killer. With the body count at 26, police stopped and questioned 23-year-old Wayne Williams before letting him go. Following the discovery of two more bodies and with mounting evidence against Williams, law-enforcement officials arrested him, finally putting an end to the outrage of a community.

Wayne Williams was born in 1958 in Atlanta, Georgia, to two middle-aged black schoolteachers, Herman and Fay Williams. He was a pudgy, pampered only child. But he was also an intelligent, enterprising youngster, so much so that he was featured in magazines and on television for starting up his own home-built radio station.

Williams left school at age 18. He learned how to use cameras, both for still photography and television. He used this ability to bill himself as a talent scout. One of his schemes was posing as the promoter of a pop-soul group. One would-be singer who answered Williams's offer of "free" interviews for singing careers, Patrick Rogers, was murdered.

In July 1979, when the decomposed bodies of two black teenagers, Edward Smith and Alfred Evans, were found near a lake in Atlanta, the city was apathetic about the murders. In September, when Milton Harvey, another black teenager, disappeared, the public still didn't notice. Then Yusef Bell, the gifted son of a civil rights worker, failed to come home. His body and that of Milton Harvey were found about the time that nine-year old Jeffrey Mathis vanished. Disappearing one after the other were Angel Lanier (the only victim who was raped), Eric Middlebrooks, Christopher Richardson, Aaron Wyche, and LaTonya Wilson.

By then, a year had passed and blacks nationwide believed that the murders were racially motivated. The police disagreed, believing that people would have noticed a white person snatching children in a black neighborhood.

On July 30, 1980, Earl Terrell disappeared. A month later, Clifford Jones vanished; his strangled body was found the following day. Twenty policemen were added to the task force. A reward was offered, and a curfew was imposed. Although police believed the killer to be a black teenager whom the children trusted, others held to the racial theme because only one child had been sexually assaulted. The disappearances continued: Darron Glass, Charles Stevens, Aaron Jackson, and Lubie Geter. By May 1981, 26 bodies had been discovered and one was missing. The police were discouraged, since they had done all they could to check out all the leads.

Police were close to a Chattahoochee River bridge on May 22 when they heard a splash. They questioned Wayne Williams, who was climbing into a nearby station wagon. After letting him go, they put him under surveillance. On May 24, the body of Nathaniel Cater, 27, and the body of Jimmy Payne, 21, were found in the river. Witnesses placed the newly found victims with Williams. Dog hairs on the victims' bodies matched hairs in Williams's home and car. Several black teens testified that Williams had approached them for sex. Although the evidence was circumstantial, Williams was convicted of killing Payne and Cater. In March 1982, Williams received a life sentence, and the murders ceased.

LEE WUORNOS

WUORNOS IS ACCUSED OF BEING ONE OF THE FEW
KNOWN FEMALE SERIAL KILLERS.

Compared with the frenzied reactions to the
Boston Strangler or the Night Stalker, a yearlong
series of killings near a Florida highway caused little stir.

Middle-aged male motorists were being found
dead along the corridor of U.S. Interstate 75 in
north-central Florida, but no one suspected the
highway slayer was a woman. Statistically, female
serial killers are so rare that at first Florida authorities were certain they were on the wrong track.

Two women were reported seen July 4, 1990, in
north Marion County fleeing from a wrecked car.
The automobile was traced to Peter Siems, a 65-
year-old missionary from Jupiter, Florida, who had
been missing since early June. Police, however,
remained reluctant to link the two women to anything more serious than robbery.

But when the nude body of Walter Antonio was
found near a hunting road in Dixie County on
November 19, 1990, authorities vigorously began

circulating composite sketches of the two women suspected in Siems's disappearance. Tips soon led investigators to Tyria Moore, onetime lesbian lover of Aileen ("Lee") Carol Wuornos.

Under intense questioning, Moore admitted knowledge of the highway slayings but denied participating in them. Moore then led authorities to a creek in Volusia County. There, divers found a .22-caliber revolver believed to have been used by Wuornos in the killings.

In January 1991, in the prophetically named Last Resort—a biker bar just down the street from the shabby Port Orange motel where Wuornos and Moore had been living since September 1990—police finally caught up with Lee Wuornos. She was initially charged on an outstanding 1986 warrant for carrying a concealed weapon. Following her arrest, investigators quickly tied Wuornos to seven highway killings along the I-75 corridor through forensic evidence and property stolen from the victims found in storage areas used by Wuornos.

Wuornos has since confessed to at least two of the slayings, but she strenuously contends they were committed in self-defense. One of her admitted victims was 56-year-old Charles Humphrey, a former Alabama police chief who was working as a Florida state investigator at the time he was murdered. Humphrey had disappeared September 11,

1990, while on his way to work. The following day his body was found near Ocala, Florida, riddled with seven bullet shots. The last shot, Wuornos stated, was in his head "to put him out of his misery."

Police authorities believe Wuornos met some of her victims at seedy truck stops in central Florida; others were flagged down along the highway and offered sexual favors in return for a ride. Empty condom wrappers were found in the cars of several of the slain men. Although Wuornos robbed all of her victims, prosecutors are seeking for another motive. When Marion County Sheriff's Captain Steve Binegar announced murder charges against Wuornos, he stressed that the weathered blonde "is a killer who robbed, not a robber who killed." Others close to the case have attributed Wuornos's killings to a long-standing hatred of men.

Much of Wuornos's earlier life remains shrouded in mystery. She herself has told wildly conflicting stories of her childhood and upbringing in suburban Detroit, though by any account her childhood was not easy. Her father committed suicide in prison following his conviction for kidnapping and sodomizing a child.

Most of her adult life has been spent in Florida, often either in prison or on the lam. In 1982, Wuornos was convicted of armed robbery and sentenced to three years. Soon after her release from prison, she met Tyria Moore at the Zodiac, a bar located in South Daytona, Florida. Lee Wuornos and the short, dark, heavy-set Moore were together for four years, first as lovers and then in a relationship characterized by Moore as "sisterlike." To support them, Wuornos turned to prostitution.

Wuornos's chief supporter since her arrest has been Arlene Pralle, an Ocala housewife and a born-again Christian. Pralle believes she is the only person Wuornos has truly bonded with in Wuornos's life. Meanwhile, Wuornos has sold the film rights to her story to Jackelyn Giroux, an opportunistic California producer. Florida officials, however, are working to use the "Son of Sam" law to prevent Wuornos from receiving any money should she be convicted. A sizable book contract is also in the offing, for Wuornos is alleged to be not only one of the few female serial killers but also a most talkative criminal.

ZODIAC

PUBLICITY-HUNGRY ZODIAC TOOK PLEASURE IN ANNOUNCING HIS MURDEROUS WAYS.

Police officially attribute six murders and two attempted murders in the San Francisco area between 1966 and 1969 to the Zodiac killer. But he was never caught; authors and law enforcement authorities for years have been coming up with theories that have attributed as many as 49 deaths to Zodiac, even though many of those cases have resulted in indisputable arrests.

Authorities believe Zodiac's first victim was Cheri Jo Bates, an 18-year-old freshman at Riverside City College. On the night of October 30, 1966, she left the campus library and found her car disabled. Police believe that a "Good Samaritan" offered to help but instead pulled her into some bushes, stabbed her in the chest and back, and slashed her throat.

Zodiac's relationship with the media started after Bates's death with a letter on November 30, 1966. On April 30, 1967, Zodiac sent another letter to newspapers, to police, and to Bates's father claiming that Bates had to die and warning that his wrath would continue.

He was once again silent for a long period, but he was also true to his word. Shortly before Christmas of 1968, 17-year-old David Faraday and his date, 16-year-old Betty Lou Jensen, were sitting in a parked car on a quiet road in the hills just outside Vallejo, north of San Francisco. A man crouching outside the car window pulled a gun and shot Faraday several times in the head. Jensen tried to run but was shot five times in the back with a .22-caliber automatic pistol.

Six months later, police were investigating another Lover's Lane murder. This time, Michael Mageau, 19, and Darlene Ferrin, 22, ended their July 4, 1969, date at Blue Rock Springs Park. A car pulled up and shined a bright light in Mageau's eyes, temporarily blinding him as the killer opened fire with a 9mm pistol. Mageau survived his four gunshot wounds, but Ferrin was pronounced dead on arrival at a local hospital after being hit by nine bullets.

Later that night, Zodiac was kind enough to call police and tell them that there had been a murder in the park. During the brief call, he also reminded officers that he was responsible for the Christmas killing that had occurred six months earlier.

These killings and related letters to newspapers sparked interest in the shadowy killer. On July 31,

1969, Zodiac wrote to three area newspapers. Each letter contained a handwritten note that verified his identity by providing never-publicized details of the killings. It also included one third of a cryptogram consisting of a mysterious series of letters and signs that hid his message. Zodiac said that if the newspapers did not run the message, he would expand his killing spree. The message was signed with a circle divided by a cross, which soon would become Zodiac's signature.

The cryptogram was printed, but the *San Francisco Examiner* also asked for more proof. The killer responded with a letter giving even more details, including descriptions of how the bodies were found. He also headed the letter with the phrase that soon became his expected opening line: "This is Zodiac speaking."

Zodiac's message in the newspaper was finally decoded by a high school teacher and his wife, and the public learned of Zodiac's goal—killing people so that in the afterlife they would become his slaves. Still police had no clue to his identity.

Zodiac's next attack was the first in daylight. Wearing an executioner's mask, Zodiac pulled a gun and tied up a young couple near Lake Berryessa on September 27, 1969. He then drew a knife and stabbed the man six times in the back. The man survived, but the woman did not. She had been stabbed once in the back and 23 times in the front, and the killer had taken care to inflict her wounds so that they would form the shape of a cross. Before leaving, Zodiac wrote the dates of all of his murders on the back of the man's car.

Less than two weeks passed before Zodiac struck again, this time in the city of San Francisco. He hailed a cab and, from the back seat, shot the driver. He tore a swatch of bloody clothing from the driver and fled. But, for the first time, police had a witness. Police now knew they were looking for a heavy-set man, age 20 to 25, with a reddish crew cut and thick glasses.

Letters from Zodiac started pouring in to newspapers, complete with parts of the cab driver's clothing. At one point, Zodiac terrified the entire city by threatening to shoot out the tire of a school bus and pick off the children as they exited. He also promised a new reign of killings, all of which would be masked as robberies, killings of anger, and suicides.

However, as far as police can tell, none of the killings ever took place. Zodiac was heard from again, claiming responsibility for several murders, but none was documented. Police believe other letters sent to newspapers in 1978 and signed "Zodiac" were actually from a detective who worked on the case. While many like to theorize, the fact remains that Zodiac, who was responsible for six murders, has never been caught.